HOW TO
PREACH A
PARABLE

EUGENE L. LOWRY

For Gerry —
Good being with you
this week.
Gene Lowry
25 Apr 88

HOW TO PREACH A PARABLE

Designs for Narrative Sermons

Abingdon Press
Nashville

How to Preach a Parable: Designs for Narrative Sermons

This book is printed on acid-free paper.

Lowry, Eugene L.
  How to preach a parable: designs for narrative sermons / Eugene L. Lowry.
    p. cm.
  ISBN 0-687-17924-6 (alk. paper)
    1. Preaching. 2. Story sermons. 3. Sermons, American.
  I. Title.
  BV4221.L68 1989
  251—dc 19   89-191
                                                                      CIP

MANUFACTURED BY THE PARTHENON PRESS AT
NASHVILLE, TENNESSEE, UNITED STATES OF AMERICA

In memory of

Dennis M. Willis
(1946–1986)

student—teacher—friend

Acknowledgments

My thanks go to Drs. Fred Craddock and Leander Keck and to Abingdon Press for permission to utilize their previously published sermon manuscripts. I am particularly grateful to Diana Willis, widow of Dennis Willis, for her permission to utilize his unpublished sermon. Dennis was just beginning what would have become an enormous contribution to the field of preaching in this country—cut short by his untimely death. For his name to appear on the cover in the company of Craddock and Keck is altogether appropriate.

Likewise, I want to express my appreciation for all those at Abingdon Press who have brought the book to fruition, particularly: Don Hardy, whose ideational dream it was; Robert Conn and Gregory Michael, editors who skillfully shepherded the process; Rebecca Marnhout, copy editor, whose careful and caring attention to both language and my writing has been crucial; and Ronald Patterson, former vice-president and editorial director for Abingdon and currently senior editor of church resources, whose support and guidance from opening conversation to finished product were indispensable.

Finally, to colleagues, friends, and family who have encouraged (and critiqued) my work in myriad ways, my deepest thanks.

Contents

HOW TO PREACH A PARABLE

Introduction

Two concerns give rise to this book: first, that some preachers may shy away from preaching on the parables—believing their literary form too difficult for the "average" preacher to handle, and, second, that not a few preachers believe only the rare and gifted preacher can preach narrative sermons.

It was in July of 1986, when I was teaching and preaching at the Proclamation '86 event in Nashville, that the editors of Abingdon Press expressed to me their concern that, due to feelings of inadequacy, many preachers apparently were avoiding parable preaching. They asked me if I would be willing to write a book that might allay those fears by helping preachers learn how to do it. This project is the result of their request.

Likewise, I had been experiencing a growing concern that often people seemed to relegate narrative preaching to the province of a few preachers of a "special breed"—those who were natural storytellers. I knew that couldn't be, since no one ever imagined me as a "storyteller," and yet I always preach narrative sermons. Others relegate narrative preaching to a "special occasion" kind of sermon—reserved for the handling of stories only. Perhaps the problem is that too many people—including some of those writing on the subject—confuse *story* sermons and *narrative* sermons.

The crucial issues in working on these dual concerns of preaching on the parables and narrative preaching are: How can a book be specific enough to be helpful in demonstrating how to learn the techniques, and how can a book avoid becoming too distant from the actual preached sermon?

My response is a "how-to" volume that centers on sermons that actually have been preached and that model different design options. I have chosen four sermons that will do exactly that. Likewise, I attempt to prepare the reader for the experience of the different narrative designs by walking through the preliminary sermon preparation process that eventuates in their use. All four sermons are narrative in form, and based on biblical stories. One is derived from a parable of Jesus. The other three treat biblical stories in parabolic fashion.

All of which means this book will be organized a bit differently. Instead of organizing narrative principles and techniques into a list and then enumerating them one by one or chapter by chapter, we will allow the sermons to present the narrative features as they actually emerge in the sermons themselves. We will find ourselves in the "detective" mode as we investigate closely *what* it is these preachers do and *how* they do it—even to the point of utilizing a running commentary with the sermon manuscripts.

Before experiencing the sermons, however, there are a very few preliminary matters to be named so we will know what to look for. I shall be very brief. And we will imagine our going through initial preparation process steps that will place us at the threshold of needing to choose one of the designs.

All of this is predicated on two assumptions. First, narrative preaching is not an esoteric art form reserved for the few. All of us can utilize the method—indeed, I believe, ought to. Second, the parables and other biblical stories provide particularly rich material with which to preach. Indeed, such biblical material assists us toward more powerful preaching.

PRELIMINARY ISSUES
AND ASSUMPTIONS

The Impact of Recent Biblical Scholarship

Perhaps it used to be easier to preach on the parables; at least, the task was clear in my mind when I graduated from seminary thirty years ago. I was told that a parable had a single point. The preacher's job was to find out what that point was and develop a sermon around it. Of course, we were properly admonished to note the important distinction between allegories and parables: Allegories have multiple referents; everything stands for something else. But parables have a single referent. Appropriately, I was warned that if I turned a parable into an allegory, it would become awkward and artificial, "walking on all fours" as it were.

I recall having the distinction illustrated from the New Testament. The prodigal son story is a parable, while the seed, sower, and soil narrative is technically an allegory. That is, the sower *really* is God, the seed is the Word of God, and the soil is the personal receiver of the Word. The "this really means that" character of allegory provides an infinite trap, I was told. Without discipline the preacher finally will have the rain referring to something else; surely the birds must represent something else, and so forth. I was instructed to notice that the prodigal son story, on the other hand, has only one referent, namely that the father represents God. The character of God's gracious love is hence the real subject of the sermon, whatever else may happen.

Now, however, thirty years later, we are instructed with far more elaborate, subtle, even esoteric distinctions. Not that current scholarship would remove the distinction between parable and allegory—indeed, it underscores that distinction further. Recent biblical studies suggest, for example, that a parable doesn't *have* a point, it *is* a point. Further, there is no external referent at all; the message is held in solution. Other writers help us engage in an examination of the literary structure of the story itself, and others note the metaphoric character of all language.

Wonderful things are happening in all this, and not for a moment would I discount their importance. Indeed, I utilize this research in my writing and my preaching. Unfortunately, however, one unintended result of this current scholarship is to frighten some preachers away from using the parables in their preaching. Apparently, some pastors worry that their own scholarship just isn't recent enough, deep enough, or trustworthy enough for them to see the homiletical clearing, let alone to enable their congregation's hearing of the Word.

Other preachers appear to have concluded that since so much recent scholarship deals with the intricacies of metaphor, it might just be better to leave such matters in the hands of the poets and to preach on more prosaic themes.

Still others seem to have categorized preachers into two groups, storytellers and non-storytellers, placing themselves, of course, in the latter camp. Recently I was disappointed to hear that one reviewer who had been kind in evaluating my last book, *Doing Time in the Pulpit*, then had occasion to hear me preach and concluded that I was able, apparently, to "do it" but that narrative preaching just "isn't for everybody."

I believe all these conclusions are unwarranted.

Indeed, what a shame it would be if preachers were to decide that they simply were not properly equipped to handle the parables in their preaching anymore. What a tragedy if out of false modesty or in deference to the presumed brilliance of the experts, we were to avoid some of the richest treasures the Bible has to offer for our preaching. Indeed, the matter goes even deeper than this. Whenever we utilize any biblical story for preaching purposes—the healing of the Gerasene demoniac, for example—its homiletical use is parabolic in nature. (In fact, the issues we will address here are important for whatever biblical text is used for preaching—story or not.)

Hence, one purpose of this book is simply to inquire, How does one go about developing a sermon based on a parable or other biblical story? Is it possible for ordinary preachers to engage in narrative preaching?

The Parabolic Nature of Stories

Any time a preacher launches into an illustration or a worker relates an incident from the job, a central and simple assumption is being made—that there must be something in it that makes it worth telling. That *something* is that the story means more than it says. Now, to be sure, any family may be interested in what happened at school today, but if the incident is recounted outside the family circle, there must be something more at stake.

When the preacher commences with "She walked into the flower shop to pick up some roses she had ordered, and . . . ," we all presume that the tale is not told for flower lovers only. Obviously, we anticipate that some concern about life both inside *and outside* the flower shop is going to be presented.

Often it is difficult to name exactly what we mean by "more," but we all know how it feels. If effective, the story, tale, or narrative must have within it some seed or germinal quality that does not quit with the teller's last word. Typically, we preachers have thought of it in terms of a "point" that the illustration makes or describes. Often, however, the term *point* doesn't quite do justice to the effect. It suggests something too neat and tidy.

Powerful stories *do* something, *effect* something, in ways not captured by the response "Oh, yes, I now understand the point."

Could it be that we are talking about a *connection* that gets made, a relational gestalt triggered, or some universal reality evoked? Something gets exposed, and we may nod involuntarily or break into laughter because of the shock of it. It is as though the incident inside the flower shop triggers something deep within us, larger than roses. Or the event is a kind of microcosm of human experience, and we say, "Well, that says it all!" More than that, the story captured us ever so briefly, took us into the flower shop, and we don't just hear the report about the woman's anger, we get a touch of anger ourselves.

So it was that when Jesus responded to the lawyer's question about neighborliness by launching into story with "There was a man who . . . ," he had more in mind than for the lawyer (and the rest of us) to have a good, clean definition of "neighbor." He wanted all of us *on the road* so we could *experience* the meaning of neighbor.

Without, I hope, espousing some form of reductionism that would do injustice to the experts in the field of metaphor, I suggest that the above description of story might help remove the veil from metaphorical theory. What they are talking about in specialized language has its roots in our everyday experience. Let us not be put off or baffled by talk of "in-meaning" as contrasted with "through-meaning," or respond with the accusation that they are alienating the text from its context. Let us first simply note that whatever is true about life *outside* the flower shop *is first evoked inside the flower shop*. If we become impatient to see a story's general relevance, our peripheral vision will obscure the moment of experience.

I hear this happen repeatedly in the sermons of the preacher who is "careful" to preface an illustration by alleging, first, that the story has had a profound impact upon the preacher's life, second, that it involves important consequences for us all, and, third, that, hence, it will be told with the hope that we will forgive this momentary diversion. *All I want is to be let into the flower shop!* (And I will make my own judgment about the story's relevance, anyway.)

Behind this nervous, apologetic stance is an epistemological assumption, namely, that meaning always stands outside experience, which, it seems to me, is very poor theology. This book is written with the assumption that if one cannot catch the meaning of "neighbor" from inside Jesus' story of the good Samaritan, one is not likely to discover it elsewhere.

With two additional and related assumptions, also, will we explore parables and other biblical stories: first, that stories are not cognitively void—to be used in order to rest the folks from thought or to be momentarily entertaining; and, second, that listeners typically have enough empathy and imagination that they do not have to take a trip to the Holy Land to see the Jericho road, nor be beaten up by a thief, nor even to have entered a flower shop, in order to experience the story. Indeed, the storyteller or parable preacher does not have to produce such connections of meaning; life does.

Narrativity as Sermonic Form

For those unfamiliar with my previous writings, I need to briefly explain the two meanings I intend by my use of the terms *narrative* and *story*.

So far I have utilized either term to mean *a* narrative, a particular story, such as the parable of the good Samaritan, the flower shop story, or the specific incident that occurred at work. This is the usual meaning of the term. Considered in plural form, we speak of *stories* or *narratives*. There is yet another meaning of the term.

One might notice during steady watching of the "Quincy" television series, for example, that all the episodes share a common shape. Quincy always begins with a dead body (at least one) that presents a problem for him—something strange about the death. He goes to work solving the riddle of the inexplicable death, only to have matters get worse: similarly unexplained deaths occur, he makes a series of dead-end attempts to solve the issue, the boss pressures him to get on with other pressing business, co-workers are disinterested, those who could help him only resist. Things always get worse. The climax comes when he goes out on a limb in some way (against even the good advice of his faithful assistant, Sam). And a wonderful surprise happens to him and all of us, as the riddle gets solved. It is a real breakthrough. (Note, however, that his commitment—or obsession—is a necessary but not sufficient cause for resolution. Theologically speaking, the answer always happens from the outside—things "fall into place" as a result of a revelation from "out of the blue.") Quincy's maligned integrity is vindicated, his foes are vanquished, and the world is made all the safer for his perseverance. The major characters head to Danny's "Proleptic Bar" for the celebrative denouement. At Danny's the conversation includes more than how it was that Quincy was able to "solve" the riddle and where things presently stand. The conversation always anticipates the future—how the world is altered by this turn of events.

Now, please notice that the above sequences seem *always* to happen in the "Quincy" episodes. To be sure, there is an ample supply of dead bodies, the riddles are varied, the opposition comes in differing forms, but the *principle*, the sweep of action, moving from riddle to surprising turn to better result, is constant. We are dealing here with the commonality of the plot line. Its constancy helps us have enough security to endure the suspense; the differing faces, issues, and actions keep us from saying, "When you've seen one, you've seen them all."

This commonality of process rightly can be termed *narrative*. Even when comparing two quite different television series, although they may do business quite differently, *there are constants* in terms of plot. To speak of *narrative* or *story* in this sense is quite different from referring to *a* particular narrative. (By analogy, we might note the difference between particular *medicines* and *medicine* in the sense of the healing arts.)

Sometimes when writers in the field of preaching speak of *narrative sermons*, people think they mean either, one, that every sermon ought to be chock full of stories, or, two, that every sermon ought to be one long story. But there is another option. The intended meaning of the term *may well be* that the writer thinks all sermons ought to follow a narrative sequence (of opening conflict, escalation, reversal, and proleptic closure).

(Indeed, there are writers in the field of homiletics who have not grasped this second meaning of the term *narrative* and hence continue to slay the wrong presumed dragons.)

So, the term *narrative* (or *story*) *may mean* a particular story; for example, "There was a man who had two sons. . . ." *Or*, on the other hand, the term *narrative* (or *story*) *may mean* the underlying thread or plot line typical of oral narration. It may be helpful to think of the first meaning of narrative as narrative *content* and the second as narrative *form*. (The fit here is not exact but perhaps helpful.) In any case, I will use the term *narrative* when speaking of narrative form and *story* when referring to a particular narrative. Also, I will try to be clear about those more technical moments when the term *narrative* has the added meaning of a story as told through narration.

There are two particular reasons why this matter is important. The first is that I happen to be one of those writers who believe in narrative preaching (in the sense of *form*). That is, I see every sermon as an event-in-time, which (as I have indicated in previous writings) moves from opening disequilibrium through escalation of conflict to surprising reversal to closing denouement (in which the table of life gets set for us in a new way by the gospel).

In this sense, all preaching that utilizes this kind of sermonic process (even if obscured somewhat by big Roman numerals) fits the category—at least in part. Such a narrative sermon *may* in its totality involve the movement of a single story, or it may include several short anecdotes or illustrations. But whether or not it involves either of the above, it is a narrative sermon *if* it follows the process of narrativity (from disequilibrium to resolution). I happen to believe that such narrative process sermons (narrative form) proceed on the most sound principles of preaching that I know.

Since I have already treated this subject in *The Homiletical Plot* (in which I attempt to show *how*) and in *Doing Time in the Pulpit* (in which I try to explain *why*), we will not explore this matter further now—except to anticipate that in section 2, "Narrative Sermon Designs," we will be dealing precisely with this kind of sermon.

The second reason for differentiating between *story* and *narrative* is for clarity in understanding the current literature about story and narrative. There are many people writing about the use of stories, biblical and otherwise, in preaching. I agree with much that is being said. Yet many readers—and a few writers—seem not to understand the distinction being used here and hence believe that those of us who are interested in *narrative* preaching are really suggesting that preaching ought to be in the form of a story only. They presume that a very narrow view of preaching is being advocated as normative and react to what they view as the severe limitations of such a view. Often a discussion will follow about whether a story can fully convey this or that, or whether one needs propositional argument as well, and so on, which is to blur if not miss altogether what theorists of narrative preaching may be all about. Certainly, such a meaning of narrative preaching is not what I have in mind.

Relation of Text and Sermonic Form

A further reason for us to discern the distinct meanings of the terms *narrative* and *story* is that particular biblical stories (parables and other accounts) come in all kinds of shapes and sizes, forms and configurations. Some are long, some short, some share the comedy of the gospel's grace, others the tragedy of judgment; some are like an opening riddle, others involve clear admonition. Obviously, one cannot handle these different kinds in exactly the same way homiletically. To do so would result in a sermonic painting-by-numbers. For example, the prodigal son/elder son story is quite involved (some preachers choose to form two sermons out of the text), while the immediately preceding story of the lost coin is short and simple by comparison. To handle both stories in the same way (in terms of narrative shape) would be unproductive.

Quite shortly, we will see how one goes about choosing from several options, which provide needed variety in the treatment of different biblical stories. For now I suggest we utilize a simple analogy for the sake of preliminary clarity about the difference between *story* and *narrative*.

Imagine you are taking a trip in a car. The car is specific in content—made of various kinds of stuff: nuts, bolts, fenders, one engine, two doors, and one steering wheel. You could be driving another one, of course, but this is the one you're in. But the car is involved with more than people and a few pieces of luggage. It is filled with motion—wheels turning, gas burning, and ultimately a distance traversed. The trip is comprised of car stuff *plus* the context of the highway, movement and destination.

One time you might be in a lean, fast car, which would alter the nature of the trip. Or again, you might choose a wide, comfortable one, which assists in the trip being what it is. But the trip is the *form* the car is helping to achieve. It is possible to imagine an automobile trip in which one never gets out of the vehicle. More likely, the car is basic in making the trip possible, but folks will get out for a bus tour, ride down a canyon on a mule, take a brief spin in a speedboat, and spend nights in motels. Whether the vehicle is indistinguishable from the experience—save for analysis—depends on the trip envisioned.

So the biblical story is the specific content—the vehicle. The sermon is the form. In the case of a parable of Jesus, the parable happens to be the story involved in the narrative process trip (with a plot line from here to there.) Of course, the relation of story to narrative flow is far more intimate than that of a car to a trip. The story is not so much sitting on the top of narrative form as much as it is becoming one with or moving through the narrative process. Likewise, just how dominant the story is in the narrative flow depends on the nature of the story and the purpose of the sermon (different cars and different trips).

All of this will become manifestly clear through our experience with four sample sermons, which we will explore in section 2.

DESIGNS FOR THE
NARRATIVE SERMON

Prelude

Choosing from the several options of sermonic design is not the first step in the formation of a narrative sermon—it is the central task, both in the sense of importance and in terms of when it happens within the sermon preparation process. Hence, in order to consider the options we must first review the steps that lead directly to that central task of sermon formation.

The preacher begins the preparation process by gaining an effective familiarity with the text that will be utilized. Otherwise, form will not follow function. This "effective familiarity" involves a peculiar blend of knowledge and mystery, of grasping and being grasped, of managing and being led. It is easier to say what it is not than what it is, although most preachers know when it is happening well.

Numerous traps await the preacher in the sermon preparation process. Several can be identified easily. In the process of exploring several of these traps to be avoided, we will begin the more difficult job of naming the positive signs of being on target in the preparation process.

Because the first task in sermon preparation is to *listen to the text*, it is important not to be upstaged by expert helpers who will give us answers to questions we have yet even to ask. I believe too many preachers (lectionary followers in particular) turn much too quickly from a first reading of the text to brief commentaries, so easily available. Understand, I am not quarreling with exegetical assistance. Indeed, without it text turns to pre-text, and what might have been biblical preaching turns into a manipulative form of topical preaching. Exegetical assistance is an indispensable part of biblical preaching. But there is a time and a place for it, and it is not now.

Since our first task is *hearing*, it is important to position ourselves in such a way that we really can be open to listening. Our intention to *plan a sermon* is commendable—and inevitable, for Sunday is fast approaching. Yet our task at this early moment in the preparation process should be to set aside our intentionality in favor of the possibility of inadvertent surprise. We already have enough trouble imposing our own agendas onto a text. Right now, let's not impose others' agendas either.

Instead, I suggest we read the text out loud, repeatedly, and in as many different translations and paraphrases as we have available. It is particularly helpful to read the text in the original language, if possible—not yet for purposes of exegetical scrutiny, but for the purpose of hearing. I suggest delaying word study at this point, unless something jumps out and slaps us in the face. Right now we are trying to be impacted by the *whole*. Dissecting the parts will come later.

It is important to stay out of the driver's seat at this stage. Our present need is to be accosted, confronted. Does this mean that all we can do is wait quietly and prayerfully for the Word to drop by? I think not. There is something we can *do* that by its nature can help keep us out of the driver's seat and assist the possibility of our being confronted. *We can look for trouble.*

What is there about the text that does not seem to fit? Is there anything strange here? "Ideological suspicion" does not always feel comfortable for us, particularly when we are included in its object. After all, we are handling the sacred Word; we are paid for answers supplied. But "suspicion" in its positive sense of *probing uncertainty* is precisely what can be helpful here. *Trouble* in, around, with, and about the text is often the occasion for a fresh hearing. In leading lectionary workshops, I often ask the participants to gather in small groups and look for what is *weird* in the passage. Anything is helpful at this point, if it breaks us loose from the usual, the easily accepted, the routine and timid truth that will not change lives.

Sometimes the "trouble" will not show itself until we have read the previous two chapters of the text *and* the following chapter as well. Our particular text, after all, did not come out of a vacuum. Its placement in the biblical sweep was the result of someone's conscious strategy.

We are looking for trouble, for textual issues. As we are confronted by them we begin, like any good detective, to research them. Word study, introductions to the book as found in a good commentary, comparisons with parallel or conflicting passages—all the resources of solid exegetical work will now be in order. Now we are on the kind of trail for disclosures that give life and vitality. But note the difference between exploring a text to find its *answer* and exploring a text to pursue its *problem*. The first puts us in command. The second, while prompting similar exegetical work, positions us as *investigator* rather than as *explainer*. Instead of placing us in a nice tidy little circle with God and the text as over against the listener, we become the first listener.

In all of this we are headed toward the first of three major moments in the sermon preparation process. This first major moment is to answer the question, *What is the focus of the text?*

The question of *focus* is born out of the need to know what is at stake here, what biblical issue or issues needed to be addressed in the first place. If narrative process is to be followed, the sermon will begin—one way or another—with a discrepancy, a conflict, an ambiguity needing resolution. Now, sometimes the biblical text does not appear to name a specific issue but rather contains a fairly straightforward declaration of some kind, which means the preacher needs to look before and after the specific text in order to find the focus—or, perhaps, imaginatively to the likely reaction of the original receivers or even of next Sunday's congregation.

The other two major moments in sermon preparation come in answering the questions, What will be the sermon's fundamental *turn*? and, What will be the sermon's basic *aim*?

Although at this preliminary stage in the sermon's preparation attempting to answer these two questions is probably premature, it is helpful to identify them enough to be able to anticipate their purpose and requirements.

The question regarding sermonic *turn* arises also out of my understanding of narrative process. Plots should never end quite as expected, and hence there is a natural anticipation on the part of the listener about the decisive turn that will make all things new. (For example, Quincy goes out on a limb, and Jesus reverses the lawyer's question.) Sometimes the decisive homiletical turn is provided explicitly in the biblical story. The prodigal son "came to himself" and *turned home*. Sometimes the decisive turn is not clearly visible within the story line of the text. In the case of one of the sermons to be presented later in this book, the fundamental turn comes in a previous passage. Sometimes the turn will surface as the preacher imagines the anticipated reaction to the biblical story.

All of which is to say that at this point in the preparation process, we need only to note that somewhere it must appear. We will be looking for it as we move into further exploration of the text (and with the specific design options that will be suggested). Indeed, *where* the turn occurs will help determine *which* narrative sermon model the preacher will choose.

The last major moment in the sermon preparation process is to determine the sermon's purpose or aim—that is, what do I hope to have happen as a result of the sermon having been preached? There is a difference in asking about a sermon's *message* and inquiring about a sermon's *aim*. But we are a bit ahead of ourselves since the naming of sermonic aim generally comes fairly late in the sermon preparation process.

Three major moments, then, or three major preparation tasks are fundamental to a sermon: *focus, turn,* and *aim*. Before identifying the various narrative sermon design options, we will be concentrating on the first: the sermon's focus, or textual issue.

The perceptive reader will note that my choice of key questions or norms has *not included* the one probably favored by most writers. In such a book as this, one can generally expect to be told that the preacher must settle on a *theme* and even must state it in a single sentence. In our present case that would seem appropriate at this stage in the preparation process. Why have I chosen *focus, turn,* and *aim* instead of *theme*?

The reasons are multiple and involve further preparation traps that need to be avoided. First, however, we need to note the important goal that the theme sentence attempts to accomplish. I see its primary goal as providing precision of homiletical purpose. Indeed, through the years I have heard altogether too many sermons (some of them mine) that have wandered all over God's creation looking for a place to land. Sometimes the preacher's desperation (and the listeners' as well) can be "solved" only by a lengthy closing summary prayer.

Homiletical precision is, of course, required. The question is how to achieve it. Although often recommended as the answer, theme sentences also provide potential problems.

First, a theme sentence tends to propositionalize the sermon. The sermonic goal often becomes narrowed to an educational aim: to inform, to clarify, to apply, to amplify. And then we measure our success in terms of having "gotten it across"—a very telling phrase. In the preparation process it is often true that the sooner we settle on a theme, the more likely the listener will have to settle for a report.

Second, except in unusual hands theme sentences often have the effect of turning off the mind. The reason is simply that it names next Sunday's event in terms of resolution. Lost is the torque of juxtaposition. My experience is that most students who operate with the use of a theme sentence operate deductively as soon as the theme sentence is named. The probing sense of inquiry is lessened, the focus narrowed to thoughtful and careful articulation of the "message." Now, obviously, this does not always happen. There are those who can utilize the technique with fine effect, but generally they are those whose thinking is wonderfully weird, who are able to see resolution and yet still keep the doors of the mind open. But for many, the comfort of resolution is too good to set aside for further engagement with an issue.

The major difference, then, between my advice and others' is that I attempt to achieve the important goal of precision by how I ask the sermonic *question* and how I name the sermonic *purpose* rather than by how I state the sermonic *answer*. Hence, I draw the readers' attention to *focus* and *aim* rather than *theme*. There is another trap here as well.

I believe there is an amazing kind of split personality among us preachers (and little wonder). Among the numerous hats pastors are called upon to wear, two are particularly important in the preaching event. One is that of scholar, the other, homiletician. Unfortunately, most of us have endured the experience of hearing both the scholar who could not (or would not) preach and the preacher who could not (or would not) do the homework. Perhaps they can be described as "those who have something to say but don't know how to say it, and those who know how to say it but have nothing to say."

It is necessary for us to be able to be both scholar *and* homiletician, to *do* the biblical homework and to be able to accomplish the sermonic task. *Yet this is not enough.* What is crucial is to wear both hats *throughout* the sermon preparation process. Indeed, the task at hand at one time may be biblical homework and at another time the task may be sermonic formation. Yet in each case the other is *also* present.

Those who suggest a thematic statement in the sermon preparation process often place it exactly between biblical work and sermon formation. The unintended result is to divide the work, with the whole process unwittingly imagined as an hourglass on its side: biblical work narrowing toward the thematic sentence, which then opens into sermon formation. I believe this to be an unnecessary, even counterproductive, division of labor.

How often it has been true for me that if I had to write a theme statement, I would be unable to name it until almost the end of the preparation process. Moreover, once a theme sentence is produced, the preacher tends to move into the driver's seat and take charge.

In contrast, experienced novelists and other narrative artists are likely to note that they never quite know where the story will go—or should go—until they follow it to the end. We, too, need to maximize our capacity to keep open throughout the preparation process. The theme sentence seems not to encourage that openness. As a result, we will concentrate on the imagined use of a *focus* statement, that is, on the basic textual issue at stake. Later we will move to the questions of *turn* and *aim*.

So the preparation has more than commenced, textual trouble has been explored, the text's focus has been named at least preliminarily, significant biblical exegesis has been engaged, the sermonic aim has begun to be sensed, and the question of sermonic form now has become the central issue.

What are the options, and how will I choose one? It may be helpful to pause long enough to recall that the present task is to imagine the text as a story that is going to traverse through a narrative format, like a car on a trip. The relation of the sermon's vehicle, the story, and the narrative shape, the trip, is both intimate and variable, as we shall soon see. Sometimes the story is always the present context of what is being said. Sometimes the story recedes into the background to such a degree that the listeners temporarily "forget" the vehicle that got them to this point. Again, different vehicles produce different trips. The four options below reflect several shapes or designs—different ways that substance and form, story and flow, particular story and narrativity, might relate to each other.

Four Options

The four designs we are going to consider are *running the story, delaying the story, suspending the story,* and *alternating the story.* Let us briefly identify the basic characteristics of each.

Running the Story

This design for turning a text into a narrative sermon is the simplest to grasp, in principle. Fundamentally, it consists of following the biblical story (parable or narrative account) through the actual flow provided by the biblical text itself. Of course, the preacher will highlight, elaborate, amplify, and creatively enflesh certain portions while moving through the text. Nonetheless, the shape of the text will be the shape of the narrative sermon. That is what I mean by *running the story.*

Delaying the Story

Sometimes the emergence of the biblical text into the sermonic event needs to be delayed. Perhaps the text contains the resolution to the sermonic issue. Sometimes there are pastoral reasons to begin a sermon with a current congregational concern, which then will turn to the text for resolution. This is a particularly good option when the biblical text happens to be fairly short and uncomplicated. Or again, when the biblical passage is so well known as to have lost its surprise or its power, delaying its use by beginning with other material can be very helpful. The other material may provide a new context of meaning that will serve to empower the text anew. Whatever the reason for delaying the use of the biblical text, when this is the form the sermon takes, I call it *delaying the story*.

Suspending the Story

One of the most often used narrative sermonic designs is the *suspending the story* form. It is characterized by beginning with the text—just as in the *Running the Story* design—except that something happens somewhere along the way. Typically, the biblical story line runs into trouble. Perhaps Jesus makes a strange turn along the way, which simply cannot be fathomed: "Why would he say a thing like that?" Of course, sometimes such a question is posed by the preacher, and the answer is somehow to be found within the story itself, in which case the sermon will probably continue to follow the *running the story* design. But *if* in fact there seems no way to negotiate the "trouble" and still remain within the biblical text, then the preacher will move away from the text in a decisive, major way—which is precisely why I have chosen to use the term *suspend*. It may be that the preacher will move to a contemporary situation in order to "find a way out." Perhaps another text will do the trick. Maybe a flashback to a previous section of the biblical material (such as a previous chapter) will provide a clue to resolution. It is possible that sharing a major piece of exegetical research will be required.

But, whether a flashback, a flash-forward, or a flash-out is required, the technique of temporarily leaving the central biblical text in the middle of the story line will be called *suspending the story*. Perhaps it has become obvious that the assumption here is that the preacher will indeed return to the central text for the finishing of the sermon. It is possible to imagine the sermon never returning to the text; in such a case we likely would use a different design label to describe it. For example, were you to use two major texts in a single sermon, suspending the story line of text A midway and using text B to complete the sermon, such a sermon would better be called *delaying the story*, since text B is really the defining text. All of this will become quite clear with our examination of an actual sermon of this type.

Alternating the Story

In this particular narrative sermon design, the story line of the text is divided into sections, episodes, or vignettes, with other kinds of material filling in around the biblical story. Sometimes I have heard biblical narrative sermons include a contemporary story running parallel to the text. The preacher alternates the telling, generally beginning with the text and then moving to the other. It may be that the text is interspersed with other kinds of sermonic material. (Unfortunately, it is easy to recall poor examples of this particular design. If you have ever heard a preacher tell part of a biblical story, then generalize its "moral," then tell some more of the biblical story, and then generalize again, you can at least image the form. I will not be recommending this kind of poor example.) When the *alternating the story* design is used well, it is both a fascinating and a powerful form of narrative preaching.

These, then, are the four designs for biblical narrative preaching: *running the story, delaying the story, suspending the story*, and *alternating the story*. No doubt others could be named, yet my experience is that just about any biblical narrative sermon I have heard can be described by means of these four designs.

Our Method

Rather than discuss the four options in detail and then illustrate them, we are going to *experience* them and then discuss them. This method is a bit "untidy," in that issues will emerge from the actual flow of the sermons rather than our prior topical structuring.

I suggest that we imagine we are in a place of worship. It is now time for the sermon. Moving to the pulpit is the preacher, who will be Dr. Fred B. Craddock, Dr. Leander E. Keck, The Reverend Dennis M. Willis, or myself. In order to gain some limited sense of the oral/aural event, *I ask you to read the sermon manuscript out loud,* not silently. I want you to have the feel of the words in your ears.

Then, after we *have heard* the sermon, imagine that we are moving to a side room for a discussion of the sermon event. I will take us through the sermon process with a running commentary to indicate what I perceive to be the preacher's methods of sermon formulation, and then I will summarize the homiletical features involved.

Running the Story

It is time, then, to experience a model sermon of the first type of design. You will note by the time the scripture passage is read that the biblical story is fairly complex, lengthy and complete. As a result, the preacher will not need to transcend the story for contextual data or contemporary analogy in any major way. Almost everything will be incorporated into the story itself.

Essentially, the biblical story *is* entirely the sermon, and the sermonic telling, therefore, will be more easily negotiated than the kind in which the preacher has to enter the story, then transcend it for explanation or other material, then reenter its flow, and so on.

Listen, then, for our preacher, the late Reverend Dennis Willis, *running the story.*

(*Please read out loud.*)

"Noah Was a Good Man"
by
Dennis M. Willis

Noah was six hundred years old when the flood of waters came upon the earth. And Noah and his sons and his wife and his sons' wives with him went into the ark, to

*escape the waters of the flood. . . . But God remem-
bered Noah and all the beasts and all the cattle that were
with him in the ark. And God made a wind blow over the
earth, and the waters subsided. . . . Then God said to
Noah, "Go forth from the ark, you and your wife, and
your sons and your sons' wives with you." . . . And God
blessed Noah and his sons, and said to them, "Be fruitful
and multiply, and fill the earth." . . . Then God said to
Noah and to his sons with him, "Behold, I establish my
covenant with you and your descendants after you, and
with every living creature that is with you." . . . And
God said, "This is the sign of the covenant which I make
between me and you and every living creature that is
with you, for all future generations: I set my bow in the
cloud, and it shall be a sign of the covenant between me
and the earth." . . . Noah was the first tiller of the soil.
He planted a vineyard; and he drank of the wine, and
became drunk, and lay uncovered in his tent. And Ham,
the father of Canaan, saw the nakedness of his father, and
told his two brothers outside. Then Shem and Japheth
took a garment, laid it upon both their shoulders, and
walked backward and covered the nakedness of their
father; their faces were turned away, and they did not see
their father's nakedness. When Noah awoke from his
wine and knew what his youngest son had done to him,
he said, "Cursed be Canaan;/a slave of slaves shall he be
to his brothers." . . . After the flood Noah lived three
hundred and fifty years. All the days of Noah were nine
hundred and fifty years; and he died. (Genesis 7:6-7;
8:1, 15-16; 9:1, 8-10a, 12-13, 20-25, 28-29)*

Noah was a good man. I don't know exactly what that
means to you. But it seems to me that when I meet good
people my expectations rise, and one of the burdens of
being a good man is, I suppose, that of living out our
expectations of them. Noah was a good man. So good,
in fact, that when the rest of the world seemed bent on
self-destruction God couldn't stand the thought of
losing Noah too. Noah was a good man.

See Noah on the deck of a ship: the wind blows, the waters rise, lightning flashes, clouds high, and there Noah is, his feet glued to the deck, his knees bent rolling with the rolling of the ship. His eyes squinted, but never closed, staring out into the grayness. Against hope his hands holding onto the rudder until the knuckles are white, holding on for dear life, and for lives that are dear. Below deck is the family, the family who know Noah to be a good man. There she is, holding her children in the rolling darkness, holding tight—and knowing, knowing that above her is more than a deck, above her is Noah, that good man. For Noah was a good man. The storm for all folks good and bad eventually quiets, skies open up, water recedes, and ships come to land.

And there came a day for Noah, that good man, and his family to begin anew. To start again. Noah was a good man. And you know, of course, the next significant thing the Bible relates about Noah's life. The next thing the Bible finds important to say about Noah is he got drunk. He made a fool out of himself and he puts the blame on Ham. What do you do with a drunken sailor? What do you do with a drunken man? What do you do with a drunken sailor early in the morning? What do we do with that good man, bad man, Noah?

See Noah in another time. He is lying in the darkness of his tent; his eyes are closed, but he is awake. He fears to open his eyes . . . he fears that the darkness of the tent will not be dark enough to hide the litter in his life, scattered about the floor of the tent. To hide the brokenness of his living like a shattered family picture tossed upon the floor. There in a corner face down is a plaque to Captain Noah. "We would sail with you anywhere," and he dares not see that. Noah, his eyes still closed, prays: "Oh, God." And translated from the original Hebrew, I think that means: "Please don't let it happen again. Please don't let it be true, either fix it, or let me die. Please God!"

Perhaps it was too dark in the tent, but Noah heard no answer. But in the distance somewhere he hears other people rising, other people meeting life, other people beginning, and he groans and he knows that he must open his eyes. He must be about the day. He can't let them find him this way. In the distance he hears cheerful voices and he hates them. In the distance he finds people who don't seem to mind life, and he rues them. He opens his eyes, and for a moment wishes to praise God with gladness because the darkness still hides the shatteredness around him, the brokenness and the filth. And before Noah can sit up he begins to take deep breaths—not because he enjoys the air—but to keep his stomach down.

The noises outside are more lively now and fear is greater than his pain, and slowly and painfully he creeps to a sitting position and he prays: "Oh God." Which translated, I think means: "I didn't want it to be this way and it hurts. I wanted to stop; make it stop. Fix it, or let me die." Maybe the noises outside are too loud for God's voice to get through. For Noah tries to hold himself together—and begins to think.

It's hard for Noah sometimes to tell the difference between a memory and a dream, or just a wishful thought. He is not quite sure, but it seems as if, perhaps, maybe, he passed out last night before he finished the wine. I mean there is a chance, there is always a chance. If there is a God in heaven there has to be some wine left somewhere, and against his will he looks around the tent.

Hastily moving over some objects he does not want to see, he sees there against the wall a wine skin. They all look alike. It's hard to tell. And Noah prays: "Oh, God," which translated, I think, means: "Let there be enough. Just let there be enough to get me around and to get me up, to get me through. Please Lord, I don't want to get drunk. I promise, I won't get drunk. Just let there be enough to get me started, to get me around, to clean things up before they see, before they find out. Let there be enough." But he is already crawling toward the wine skin and he doesn't hear God answering. He lifts the wine skin and, sweet Jesus, it's not empty. And he cradles it to himself and holds it against himself, and is warmed by its coldness. He uncaps it, smells it and chokes.

There is a song by the Gatlin Brothers about a bunch of winos who go down to the Helping Hand, and they get saved and fed. Not sure which is most important. Then they go out on the street and begin hitting up folks for a little money to get through. At midnight one of them has scored, and they gather in a circle in an alley holding a bottle of Mogen David—which very communion-like they pass around one to the other. At about midnight the warmness hits and they begin to sing their midnight chorus, "Oh Mother, be Mogen David up in heaven? Oh, Lord, that's all I want to know. Will there be Mogen David up in heaven? Sweet Jesus, if not who the hell wants to go." Which is a way of saying: "Will there be a balm in Gilead?"

There is no balm for Noah. For he knows full well as he holds that wine skin that one sip is too much, and a thousand won't be enough. And so he prays the only prayer he knows. He says: "Oh, God." Which translated means: "Let me keep it down. Please don't let me throw up, not yet, not for a while." And he lifts the wine skin to his lips as he pats his hair back and forth—and he drinks that poison.

I don't like Noah very much. I guess you can tell that I kinda think he is a self-pitying wretch that creates his own problems. I just don't like him. But what happens next is too hard to bear. For the next thing to happen to Noah is the worst thing that will ever happen in Noah's life. There is nothing worse for Noah. If he lives another 600 years he will never again have to face anything worse.

The wine skin at his face, the wine pouring down both sides of his throat, and the tent flap flies open and light floods the tent. All the shadows that hid the filth and hid the brokenness are chased away. All the shadows that hid Noah are gone. And there silhouetted in the door of the tent is Ham, his baby. And the hardest thing, the worst thing that will ever happen to Noah in his life is to look into the face of his baby and see written there disgust and pity. And Noah does the only thing Noah can do. I don't like Noah, but I don't blame him at this point for what else can he do. He exercised the only option he had. He said: "Damn you Ham, damn you for seeing me like this. Damn you for knowing me for what I am, and damn you Ham."

Ham is the only hero in the story. Noah's balm. Ham is one of those people who are born to bear curses. He leaves you though. He goes to take his curse to live in a far country. I suppose that's best. I mean the only option he had was to stay and watch his Daddy die. No, far countries are filled with heroes carrying curses from home. Noah prays: "Oh, God." Which translated I think means: "How did it happen? How did it come to this? Why can't I go after my baby? Why can't I make it right?"

"Maybe, Lord, maybe, I just peaked early. I think of my days on the ship and I was good. Wasn't I good? Lord, I was good. But I ain't on the ship no more. Lord, if you don't understand how much it hurts to put on my Captain's hat . . . if you don't understand how much it shames me when they call me Capt'n . . . then you will never understand just how badly I'm going to mess up today."

The rest of the family, they don't follow Ham. You know what they do, don't you? I suppose we need to recognize that they are a part of Noah's disease, and they, too, are caught by denial and that they have no options either. But what they do . . . they won't even look at it. Oh, certainly he gives them the phrases. Certainly he tells them everything will be all right . . . that they're going to get his blessings. They won't even look. They back into the tent and then they cover it up.

What did *he* do? I wish I could go on with that story, but you see the problem is the Bible does not tell us what happened. We don't know what happened. We don't know where Noah ended up. We truly don't know what happened. But we do know, we do know what could have happened. Maybe he just got sick and tired of being tired and sick. Or maybe, it got to the point he couldn't get down to the dock to watch the ships. Or maybe he just forgot to remember it. Maybe he got to remember it wasn't always like that—that there was a time that he and God were like that. That close—that interdependent. There was time he could talk to God in prayers of more than two syllables. Maybe he got to thinking about those conversations he and God had. Maybe he was out walking and one morning just thinking about it, he got to look into the skies and saw a rainbow and remembered that a rainbow was a sign. He searched his memory to try and remember what he was supposed to feel when he saw a rainbow. What he was supposed to remember. Then it dawned on him that a rainbow was not a sign for Noah. The rainbow was a sign for God. That when God looked down he would see people through rainbows all filled with color and pretty, and God would remember that people are not made for destruction. If Noah could remember that.

If Noah could just . . . if Noah could get that far then maybe, just maybe, he could come to realize that he was powerless over alcohol and his life had become unmanageable. Ah, sweet Jesus, if he could get that far. If he could get that far. If he could hold on for just a moment and maybe he could just come to believe that a power greater than himself could restore him to sanity. If he could get that far he wouldn't have to hold on to it for the rest of his life. He would only have to hold on to it for one day at a time. If he could get that far he could make a decision to turn his will and his life over to the care of a God who sees people through rainbows bright and colorful and pretty and made for creation. Made to be fed by a God who cares so much that God transforms the Divine body into bread that we can eat and into a wine that anybody can drink.

This sermon is a good example of the *running the story* method. The forward motion of the text became the forward motion of the sermon. Although the preacher included a couple of "memory moments" that flashed back to earlier times, they were nonetheless, *inside* the present experience. The only time Willis left the story was for an ever-so-brief contemporary illustration.

In order to understand more fully the various methods Willis utilized in this sermon, we are going to take a closer look, facilitated by a running commentary. In it I will attempt to name some of what he is doing and how. This running commentary is similar in form to the biblical exegetical material we are accustomed to reading in our biblical work. Perhaps we could call this a *homiletical exegesis*. After this, I will provide a summary of the narrative features that have emerged from the commentary.

Running Commentary

Noah was a good man. I don't know exactly what that means to you. But it seems to me that when I meet good people my expectations rise, and one of the burdens of being a good man is, I suppose, that of living out our expectations of them. Noah was a good man. So good, in fact, that when the rest of the world seemed bent on self-destruction God couldn't stand the thought of losing Noah too. Noah was a good man.

The sermon starts with the story. Although the beginning sentence *seems* a transcendent conclusion, actually it is the opening conflict—coming as it does with the listeners just having heard the reading of the drunken episode account. After that scripture lesson, how could the preacher call him good? Then after a one-sentence step-away about good people's burden of others' expectations, he alleges again that Noah was a good man. He even notes God's agreement. Hence, the opening ambiguity is posed by the uncertain connection of the words "good" and "burden" juxtaposed with the textual account.

See Noah on the deck of a ship: the wind blows, the waters rise, lightning flashes, clouds high, and there Noah is, his feet glued to the deck, his knees bent rolling with the rolling of the ship. His eyes squinted, but never closed, staring out into the grayness. Against hope his hands holding onto the rudder until the knuckles are white, holding on for dear life, and for lives that are dear. Below deck is the family, the family who know Noah to be a good man. There she is, holding her children in the rolling darkness, holding tight—and knowing, knowing that above her is more than a deck, above her is Noah, that good man. For Noah was a good man. The storm for all folks good and bad eventually quiets, skies open up, water recedes, and ships come to land.

Note that Willis doesn't argue the case with logic; he simply drops us into the middle of the scene, with its sharp physical images evoking the experience. Conflict is escalated before the paragraph is completed, as Willis moves the description of Noah's character from his own allegation to the report of the family. By now the listener has heard several character references: the preacher, God, and Noah's family. The tension is lessened a bit by the preacher's anticipation of the storm's final end, but not for long.

And there came a day for Noah, that good man, and his family to begin anew. To start again. Noah was a good man. And you know, of course, the next significant thing the Bible relates about Noah's life. The next thing the Bible finds important to say about Noah is he got drunk. He made a fool out of himself and he puts the blame on Ham. What do you do with a drunken sailor? What do you do with a drunken man? What do you do with a drunken sailor early in the morning? What do we do with that good man, bad man, Noah?

Wisely, the preacher knows that if you end the storm bringing resolution to the danger and safety for the family, you had better introduce conflict of some other kind. So it is time to "start again," and promptly Noah is drunk. The tension gets deeper—enough that Willis now stands with one foot inside the story and one foot out, observing the facticity of the story. Such phrases as "the Bible relates" and "What do you do?" involve *looking at*, while "he got drunk" and "puts the blame on Ham" are *standing inside* phrases.

Our preacher knows not to stay too long with one foot outside the story and hence uses the proper name "Noah" to get fully inside again.

See Noah in another time. He is lying in the darkness of his tent; his eyes are closed, but he is awake. He fears to open his eyes . . . he fears that the darkness of the tent will not be dark enough to hide the litter in his life, scattered about the floor of the tent. To hide the brokenness of his living like a shattered family picture tossed upon the floor. There in a corner face down is a plaque to Captain Noah. "We would sail with you anywhere," and he dares not see that. Noah, his eyes still closed, prays: "Oh, God." And translated from the original Hebrew, I think that means: "Please don't let it happen again. Please don't let it be true, either fix it, or let me die. Please God!"

We find ourselves inside the tent (with Noah and the preacher). Watch now how Willis uses physical detail to draw deeper descriptions and cause greater complications. He understands the parabolic capacity of any story and connects "litter of his life" to "floor of the tent." He might have assumed we would make the connection but chooses an imagistic tease to be sure, and accomplishes the task without distancing himself or us from the thread of the story. The plaque accomplishes two important sequential purposes here. First, it helps us remember Noah's good qualities, which might become lost in this drunken scene. A less skilled preacher might have lectured us to remember that God has chosen Noah and that though drunk now he is nonetheless a person of worth, and so on. Instead, Willis gives us a plaque that keeps us in the movement of the story. Second, by means of this effective detail the narrative quality of escalating tension is kept alive. If we decide Noah is no good, the tension drops. The plaque increases the tension.

Perhaps it was too dark in the tent, but Noah heard no answer. But in the distance somewhere he hears other people rising, other people meeting life, other people beginning, and he groans and he knows that he must open his eyes. He must be about the day. He can't let them find him this way. In the distance he hears cheerful voices and he hates them. In the distance he finds people who don't seem to mind life, and he rues them. He opens his eyes, and for a moment wishes to praise God with gladness because the darkness still hides the shatteredness around him, the brokenness and the filth. And before Noah can sit up he begins to take deep breaths—not because he enjoys the air—but to keep his stomach down.

The plot thickens with the first explicit reference to the outside world, with other people in it, people who make his situation even worse. Wisely the preacher understands that if the listeners gain too much distance from Noah, we will draw moral judgments and find resolution prematurely. One effective way to prevent this is to keep us just behind Noah's eyes, perceiving the world as he did. The result is empathy. And just when there is a mild release by the "positive" phrase of drawing "deep breaths," we are shocked to discover why. We should note here that we are being kept off balance but not confused. Likewise, the preacher allows us to decide again whether God did not answer the prayer or whether the answer simply was not heard.

The noises outside are more lively now and fear is greater than his pain, and slowly and painfully he creeps to a sitting position and he prays: "Oh God." Which translated, I think means: "I didn't want it to be this way and it hurts. I wanted to stop; make it stop. Fix it, or let me die." Maybe the noises outside are too loud for God's voice to get through. For Noah tries to hold himself together—and begins to think.

It's hard for Noah sometimes to tell the difference between a memory and a dream, or just a wishful thought. He is not quite sure, but it seems as if, perhaps, maybe, he passed out last night before he finished the wine. I mean there is a chance, there is always a chance. If there is a God in heaven there has to be some wine left somewhere, and against his will he looks around the tent.

Ever more deeply the listeners are drawn into the very interiority of Noah's consciousness—even his lament of the difference between his intention and reality. Willis doesn't tell us so; he lets Noah tell us. The tragic dilemma is no longer past tense—last night's binge; it is now present tense, and we get new detail of the fierce war going on inside him. Willis' fine capacity for creative repetition is now heard in the phrase "Oh, God!" Notice how he cues us about his narrative interpretation. He does not say that the prayer actually/literally said this; he takes responsibility for it with the phrase "which translated, *I think means.*"

Hastily moving over some objects he does not want to see, he sees there against the wall a wine skin. They all look alike. It's hard to tell. And Noah prays: "Oh, God," which translated, I think, means: "Let there be enough. Just let there be enough to get me around and to get me up, to get me through. Please Lord, I don't want to get drunk. I promise, I won't get drunk. Just let there be enough to get me started, to get me around, to clean things up before they see, before they find out. Let there be enough." But he is already crawling toward the wine skin and he doesn't hear God answering. He lifts the wine skin and, sweet Jesus, it's not empty. And he cradles it to himself and holds it against himself, and is warmed by its coldness. He uncaps it, smells it and chokes.

Willis keeps us on the hook by keeping the tension between good motive and bad behavior. When lesser preachers decide that bad behavior always reflects bad motive, the sermon quickly will turn lifeless and moralistic. The power of narrative articularity is particularly evident in the phrase "warmed by its coldness." Imagine how long a paragraph of prose it would take to explain propositionally how those things we use to bring certain results actually bring the reverse. He does it with four words.

There is a song by the Gatlin Brothers about a bunch of winos who go down to the Helping Hand, and they get saved and fed. Not sure which is most important. Then they go out on the street and begin hitting up folks for a little money to get through. At midnight one of them has scored, and they gather in a circle in an alley holding a bottle of Mogen David—which very communion-like they pass around one to the other. At about midnight the warmness hits and they begin to sing their midnight chorus, "Oh Mother, be Mogen; David up in heaven? Oh, Lord, that's all I want to know. Will there be Mogen David up in heaven? Sweet Jesus, if not who the hell wants to go." Which is a way of saying: "Will there be a balm in Gilead?"

This is the one and only time Willis moves away from the story (or at least from looking *at* the story). I can well imagine he thought long and hard as to whether to include this illustration.

It does interrupt the narrative flow—which should be done only when absolutely necessary. (Note how the last line of the previous paragraph leads directly to the second sentence of the following paragraph.) Yet his purpose for including it is worthy. He wants to foreshadow the sermon's conclusion. (By *foreshadowing* is meant the technique of including an apparently innocent or passing remark that will be harvested with power later.)

> *There is no balm for Noah. For he knows full well as he holds that wine skin that one sip is too much, and a thousand won't be enough. And so he prays the only prayer he knows. He says: "Oh, God." Which translated means: "Let me keep it down. Please don't let me throw up, not yet, not for a while." And he lifts the wine skin to his lips as he pats his hair back and forth—and he drinks that poison.*
>
> *I don't like Noah very much. I guess you can tell that I kinda think he is a self—pitying wretch that creates his own problems. I just don't like him. But what happens next is too hard to bear. For the next thing to happen to Noah is the worse thing that will ever happen in Noah's life. There is nothing worse for Noah. If he lives another six hundred years he will never again have to face anything worse.*

We have already noted that the illustration breaks into the ongoing flow of the Noah narrative (and also raises some pros and cons about its inclusion). Granting the decision to include it, we should note here precisely *where* he chose to insert it. The typical preacher might decide to place it in a "break in the action," thinking it less intrusive there. Actually, the reverse is true. If one moves away from a narrative flow at a "break," the listeners may not return—surely the ultimate intrusion. Note that Willis interrupts the narrative *just before* Noah takes the drink. By suspending the action the preacher increases the likelihood of the listeners' coming back. In short, such transitions should occur at points of ambiguity, not at points of closure.

At this point, the "I don't like Noah" statement is clearly ironic, given the preacher's empathic handling of the tale thus far.

The wine skin at his face, the wine pouring down both sides of his throat, and the tent flap flies open and light floods the tent. All the shadows that hid the filth and hid the brokenness are chased away. All the shadows that hid Noah are gone. And there silhouetted in the door of the tent is Ham, his baby. And the hardest thing, the worst thing that will ever happen to Noah in his life is to look into the face of his baby and see written there disgust and pity. And Noah does the only thing Noah can do. I don't like Noah, but I don't blame him at this point for what else can he do. He exercised the only option he had. He said: "Damn you Ham, damn you for seeing me like this. Damn you for knowing me for what I am, and damn you Ham."

With powerful metaphoric tease, Willis describes Noah's external behavior and interior reality—with the same words. Notice that Noah at his very worst is portrayed as having no alternative. Hence, the listeners are kept in touch *with* Noah, rather than closing the door *on* Noah. Contrast this with the all too common preacher's moral equation: freedom of choice plus bad motive equals evil behavior plus rightful censure. Not our preacher. And we are moved not toward a condoning mood but to an empathic spirit of lament.

Ham is the only hero in the story. Noah's balm. Ham is one of those people who are born to bear curses. He leaves you though. He goes to take his curse to live in a far country. I suppose that's best. I mean the only option he had was to stay and watch his Daddy die. No, far countries are filled with heroes carrying curses from home. Noah prays: "Oh, God." Which translated I think means: "How did it happen? How did it come to this? What can't I go after my baby? Why can't I make it right?"

This brief experience of Ham is quite powerful yet filled with homiletical danger, and Willis apparently knows it. The "far countries are filled with" sentence poses one of the preacher's most potent temptations. We are caught by the powerful implications of the sentence and hence easily could be led off to another sermon altogether. The danger of a detour here arises precisely from its provocative possibilities. One more sentence and we might miss the rest of this sermon. Wisely the preacher brings us back by focusing our attention with the strength of "Oh, God."

"Maybe, Lord, maybe, I just peaked early. I think of my days on the ship and I was good. Wasn't I good? Lord, I was good. But I ain't on the ship no more. Lord, if you don't understand how much it hurts to put on my Captain's hat . . . if you don't understand how much it shames me when they call me Capt'n . . . then you will never understand just how badly I'm going to mess up today."

The rest of the family, they don't follow Ham. You know what they do, don't you? I suppose we need to recognize that they are a part of Noah's disease, and they, too, are caught by denial and that they have no options either. But what they do . . . they won't even look at it. Oh, certainly he gives them the phrases. Certainly he tells them everything will be all right . . . that they're going to get his blessings. They won't even look. They back into the tent and then they cover it up.

It is, of course, time to muse over the tragedy. This is the spot where most of us would turn to generalization with something like "What a tragedy. Here the man whom God saved by means of the ark has now messed it all up!" Willis will not allow us this release by means of distance. Instead, he has Noah muse through memory. Note the increased power when a flashback is accomplished by means of the character instead of the narrator. The result is that of a necessary pause for emphasis, an interior flashback instead of an exterior generalization (which loses grip on the story) and even an anticipation of the next stage of the story.

Meanwhile, lest the listeners forget that sin always has a

large interconnected cast of involved characters, Willis provides a nicely brief profile of their culpable response.

What did he do? I wish I could go on with that story, but you see the problem is the Bible does not tell us what happened. We don't know what happened. We don't know where Noah ended up. We truly don't know what happened. But we do know, we do know what could have happened. Maybe he just got sick and tired of being tired and sick. Or maybe, it got to the point he couldn't get down to the dock to watch the ships. Or maybe he just forgot to remember it. Maybe he got to remember it wasn't always like that—that there was a time that he and God were like that. That close—that interdependent. There was time he could talk to God in prayers of more than two syllables. Maybe he got to thinking about those conversations he and God had. Maybe he was out walking and one morning just thinking about it, he got to look into the skies and saw a rainbow and remembered that a rainbow was a sign. He searched his memory to try and remember what he was supposed to feel when he saw a rainbow. What he was supposed to remember. Then it dawned on him that a rainbow was not a sign for Noah. The rainbow was a sign for God. That when God looked down he would see people through rainbows all filled with color and pretty, and God would remember that people are not made for destruction. If Noah could remember that.

Willis attempts to reenter the narrative flow of the story but cannot. The story proper is over, except for one middle section that had been "overlooked" in his telling. We have been so engrossed in the story that we have forgotten the part about the rainbow. At least, the preacher hopes we have. And it is important for us not to notice the overlooked part, because it is the section in which the good news is to be found. If the story had been told in strictly chronological order, the good news would have come too soon, the narrative tension would have been lost, and the concluding portion would have sounded like a report about an event instead of a reenactment. My experience is that when a preacher handles a text in topical form, listeners are quick to remember what the preacher wants them to ignore. "But what about . . . ?" seems to be the order of the day when one is utilizing topical/logical argument. But when the tale is being retold, there seems to be a natural desire to "go with the flow."

Now it is time for the good news, and the missing section out of the past is made current by means of imagining future remembering. As is often the case, hope comes not from a burst of *new* news but by being grasped by good news *already known.* Note that the decisive turn, theologically, has already been made. Its manifestation is made possible on the hoped-for occasion of Noah's remembering.

> *If Noah could just . . . if Noah could get that far then maybe, just maybe, he could come to realize that he was powerless over alcohol and his life had become unmanageable. Ah, sweet Jesus, if he could get that far. If he could get that far. If he could hold on for just a moment and maybe he could just come to believe that a power greater than himself could restore him to sanity. If he could get that far he wouldn't have to hold on to it for the rest of his life. He would only have to hold on to it for one day at a time. If he could get that far he could make a decision to turn his will and his life over to the care of a God who sees people through rainbows bright and colorful and pretty and made for creation. Made to be fed by a God who cares so much that God transforms the Divine body into bread that we can eat and into a wine that anybody can drink.*

Once the decisive turn is made by means of the rainbow, the sermon is quick to close. The rainbow came, of course, by surprise—we had no way to anticipate it. And once evoked there is no turning back into the narrative. Note also how the preacher avoided the trap of explaining it in detail. In this last section the central purpose is to suggest quite briefly the resultant consequence of God's covenant via the rainbow image. Observe that the next to last paragraph contains the indicative of God's action; this last paragraph contains the imperative of its claim. Wisely Willis does not simply state the obvious, that "now Noah should get his life together by proper decisions." First he bridges indicative with imperative by saying that now Noah "wouldn't *have* to hold on" anymore.

Moreover, the preacher has given himself a real challenge—namely, to finish the sermon as powerfully crisp and imagistic as it has been all along. Typically preachers are apt to paint the story well but then conclude with pale propositional truth. Willis avoids this problem by choosing the eucharistic image of wine, which transforms powerfully the image of drinking. What once was a curse now turns to ultimate blessing.

Narrative Capabilities, Techniques, and Norms

Perhaps it will be helpful to highlight some of the narrative features included in the sermon "Noah Was a Good Man" by Dennis Willis. Some of these were mentioned in the running commentary. Now we can identify them more precisely. I perceive three categories: narrative capabilities, narrative techniques, and narrative norms. Let us see if we can name some of the aspects of narrative preaching he has taught us.

Narrative Capabilities

Widened Listening Behavior

Not only do people seem to attend to a story with heightened listening energy, as has been noted in the literature, but also, I believe, the form story takes evokes a different set of expectations and rules. For one thing, a story credibly told allows the teller greater flexibility in setting the parameters of focus. People tend to "go with the flow," with minimal imposed restrictions. If the preacher chooses to center on one aspect of a scene, listeners are not apt to complain privately that the preacher should have centered somewhere else. There are at least two reasons for this phenomenon.

First, because the narrative movement begins inductively rather than deductively, the listeners are less cued as to the "bottom line" generalization and hence not as prepared to consider different conclusions than the preacher has in mind. In the case of a deductively argued topical sermon, listeners seem more poised with objections. For example, if I suggest that the correct understanding of the Trinity is at the heart of the Christian faith, and hence about to explain its central ingredients carefully, the listeners seem to look for a way out of where I am heading. But if I notice how strange it is that one of the characters should have responded in such a way, folks seem to suspend judgment for a while, just to see what kind of "strange" it is.

Second, although part of the issue may be that of presumed authority, I believe another reason for greater openness to story has to do with aesthetic pleasure. Listening to a story well told can be fun—even when it includes matters of some pathos. Although it is a narrative art form rather than a form of the dramatic arts, storytelling seems to evoke some of the permission granted in the theater and there called the "willing suspension of disbelief." For these reasons, story allows greater flexibility for the preacher in setting the parameters of focus.

Beyond matters of focus, narrativity alters expectations regarding believability. Narrative credibility appears more compelling than rational argument. The story line's capacity to create a picture, to evoke an event, to provide action, results in a broader appeal to the mind than tightly reasoned argument. A story moves on more than one front at the same time. Hence, in our sermon above Willis did not have to defend at great length his opening claim regarding Noah's good character; he simply took us below deck for a few moments with Noah's wife. Once there, the preacher was free to paint what he wanted us to see. Because art of all kinds has the potential of grasping us rather than being grasped as ideational material, Willis was able to expose us to character judgments made before we could provide competing images. Likewise, given this potential for grasping the listener, we were kept outside the place where God's rainbow could be observed. We beheld it when the preacher was ready for the experience to occur.

The Parabolic "More"

In a previous section of this book we considered how it is that one does not tell a story about a woman who went to a flower shop for some roses unless it has a greater meaning than roses or flower shops *per se*. We are dealing here with the explicit metaphoric use of language. What this parabolic "more" means in the case of this sermon is that everything utilized in the telling of the story is, potentially, more than it says. The litter in the dark tent over which Noah stumbled means more than litter in a dark tent. So, also, the light that came through the opening when the tent flap was moved causes exposure *to happen*, not simply be reported. Not every piece of visual or auditory detail has such powerful metaphoric meaning, but because of its potential, the listener begins to pay close attention lest a central ingredient be overlooked. Some portions of a story are not intended as metaphoric language—but you can't be sure.

Moreover, the fact of the parabolic "more" means that the preacher in sermon preparation does not have to be so careful in utilizing the rules about generalization and particularization, about the concrete and the abstract. Perhaps you recall being warned to move up and down the abstraction ladder, so that people will have eggs and baskets, baskets and eggs in their listening fare. In the sweep of a story, litter on a tent floor is *both* particular and general. So are shadows and a rainbow (as well as a pigpen and a lost coin). It needs to be said, however, that although the metaphoric use of a word or phrase may help reduce the need to watch the waves of recurring particularizations and generalizations, the artistic skill required for choosing metaphors will certainly make new demands on the preacher.

Economy

In the days of my formal education—particularly high school and college—I somehow got the message that poetic language had to do with peripheral frills and embellishments. It was frosting on the cake of language. I cannot recall where I received that idea, nor remember whom to blame, but somehow it became clear to me that metaphor and other forms of "picturesque" speech were essentially ornamental—good for the sake of impression but otherwise hollow. Only later did I begin to learn not only that metaphoric speech actually carries thought, but also, indeed, that it might carry it more powerfully. What is more, poetic language can sometimes carry thought with greater economy. Willis's sermon demonstrates the point well. I noted in the running commentary how his phrase "warmed by its coldness" communicated the equivalent of several lines by means of four words—and did it with evocative power. Likewise, Jesus wanted to communicate something about a son being at the end of his rope, becoming destitute, even losing grip on his very sense of self. Jesus noted that he was sent out to "feed swine." No need to explain or amplify that for a Jew.

Having noted this powerful economy of metaphoric language, a couple of warnings are in order. First, less is more. Those who cram the story line full of obvious metaphors lose the punch because (a) listeners cannot handle the mental gymnastics involved in too many metaphoric allusions, and (b) once listeners begin to take explicit note of the preacher's overuse of the technique, they distance themselves from its effect.

Second, some preachers fall into the habit of making poetic speech by means of adverbs and adjectives instead of nouns and verbs. So we may hear about "mountain-ously doubting" and "Hitlerish speech" when the doubt needs simply to be called a mountain and the bigot depicted as a person with a swastika for a mouth. My hunch about why some inadvertently focus on adverbs and adjectives is that they really do not trust the metaphor (or the listeners) and therefore conjoin the metaphor with a "regular" noun or verb, just to be safe. The result is similar to explaining a joke. Those who got it resent the explanation, and those who didn't won't laugh now.

Narrative Techniques

Use of Repetition

Willis's fine use of repetition is most noteworthy in his use of two phrases: "Noah was a good man" and "Oh, God." In both cases he "pre-packed" them, but in different ways. We learn from him that the repeated use of a given phrase must carry what I call *increasing freight*. That is, the content of the sermon must evidence movement between any two utterances of the repeated phrase. It may be new evidence to support the image or idea; it may be another angle of view; it may be a fresh scene of action. In such a case the repeated word or phrase remains the same in content, yet it becomes further packed with power. Or the phrase utilized may itself change character as a result of the increased freight. If I were to say of someone after recounting a positive instance of behavior on his or her part, "Very clever," then provide another positive instance, followed again with the phrase, but *then* reveal a rather sneaky piece of behavior, followed by the same phrase, the result is a deepening and a turning of meaning. What is to be avoided is repeating a phrase with *no shift* in content, no movement of plot—just the repeated phrase. In this case the listener will suspect that continued use of the phrase is simply a delaying tactic while the preacher is figuring out what next to say.

Willis's other noteworthy use of repetition was the

phrase "Oh, God." The principle of increased freight was effective here as well. The difference in impact between this and the "Noah was a good man" phrase has to do with beat or rhythm. In the Noah phrase, the phrase *is* the punch line. To say it is to reap the impact of the preceding content. The "Oh, God" phrase is the upbeat instead of the downbeat; that is, its repetition sets us up for the next phrase, which is always different.

The effective use of repetition is best heard among preachers in the black tradition. Listening to tapes of the multiple forms of repetition is exceedingly helpful in developing one's technique.

There is another kind of repetition that performs other tasks for the preacher. Again, Willis demonstrates its effective use. What I have in mind here is not so much the repeated use of a single phrase as the use of variations of the same thought or image.

Sometimes what the listeners need most is *time*—enough opportunity to grasp what has been said. We who preach sometimes neglect to consider that the text, thought processes, and plots with which we have been working for most of a week reach the listeners' ears but once. We have been cogitating on it, looking at our written notations of it, and remembering it while making a hospital call. They hear it said, and then its gone—unless we find ways to repeat it. We may be operating out of a book-oriented background. It is easy for the eye to retrace some steps in case the next ideational move doesn't quite make sense. But preaching happens in time, like music heard.

It may be that the listeners' need is not to cognitively grasp what the preacher has said; it may be that time is needed for its consequences to be absorbed. Recall Willis's sermonic beginning, when the ship is rolling and Noah's wife is holding her children. Willis says; "The storm for all folks good and bad eventually quiets, skies open up, water recedes, and ships come to land." Now, one might ask, Isn't all that a bit wordy? Why not say simply, "The storm stopped"? But Willis knows that it is not enough to announce the end of the storm. If the listeners have in any sense also been in the ship and felt its rolling, they need a few seconds to get themselves together. The combination of several phrases that really say the same thing is immensely helpful. This issue bears closely on another: sermonic rhythm, that proper sense of timing that is so important. To that we shall return later.

Use of Detail

Whenever any preacher is considering the overall sweep of a biblical story to be used in a narrative sermon, among the crucial decisions to be made is the question of what to highlight in the biblical story. One cannot linger everywhere in the telling of a story. For one thing, some of Jesus' more elaborate parables (e.g., the prodigal son story) would take too long to preach if the preacher continued to keep the telling thick with detail. For another, the sermon as preached must have variety of pacing. To continue to travel at the same rate of speed becomes laborious, no matter how well a tale is told. So the preacher chooses to linger here and there in order to name the central issues, provide essential character descriptions, and establish the movement of the plot. How one utilizes detail is quite important in accomplishing these various goals. Willis's sermon not only evidences his capacity to utilize detail in the usual sense, it provides a lesson in fine tuning. In particular, Willis utilizes detail for purposes of bringing important information to the surface of the sermon, as an instrument in foreshadowing, and in order to provide an interior flashback. Briefly we will consider each of these three related purposes.

First, the use of detail for *surfacing important information:* Recall, if you will, the plaque Noah stumbled over in the darkened tent. On it was inscribed "We would sail with you anywhere." Now, why did he do that? My hunch is that in this hangover scene—which is also prelude to the next drink—Willis wanted to prevent the listeners from becoming so judgmental of Noah as to close the door of our relationship to him. The preacher needed to say something good about Noah, to help us remember that things were not always this ugly. He could have stopped the dramatic forward motion of the story line with a reminder to us that Noah was saved by God because "he walked with God" or that he was dedicated to building the ark when commanded. But these or other means would cause the preacher to leave the story for purposes of generalization. Instead, Willis inserts a plaque on the floor of the tent, which becomes part of the present action. The plot line maintains its motion, the preacher does not have to transcend the story temporarily, and the important information is inserted.

But how could Willis have been so creative as to think of such a thing? Although you and I may not have Willis's fine touch, the principle is not very esoteric. Let us imagine you are preparing a sermon for next Sunday—a narrative sermon based on a parable of Jesus'. You are about to insert some dry but important information that will force you out of the story for a moment. Instead of asking how you can get this piece in without being too obtrusive, pause for a moment and ask a different question. Is there any object, person, or action that can be imagined here? Perhaps it is a piece of furniture close by. Perhaps it is the moment of parting of prodigal son and father; the father might just say something at this moment that would surface this important data.

Actually, the key here is not in knowing to utilize this helpful technique—the key is to find that object, incident, or person that will feel credible. Generally the listeners will be generous. For example, we could have asked what a plaque was doing in the tent—but we didn't. We could imagine it; that's all it takes.

Second, *foreshadowing*—the technique used to anticipate and enhance a future major moment in a story: Foreshadowing has to do with inserting a brief, apparently innocuous detail that appears to have no great significance but that actually will figure importantly at a later stage in the telling. In preaching on the prodigal son text, I always have the father say to the son at the moment of saying good-bye, "Son, keep in touch with us . . . and, son . . . don't forget who you are." "Sure, Dad, you bet." These lines are supposed to feel like fairly typical, routine, and believable statements of parting. Actually, I intend to use the first part—the keeping in touch—to make more poignant the son's isolation in the far country. It will also foreshadow the moment when they in fact do touch again. The "don't forget who you are" line hopefully will enhance the pigpen scene when the Jewish boy winds up feeding the Gentile farmer's pigs.

In the Noah sermon foreshadowing happens in the illustration of the Gatlin Brothers' song. Willis noted "innocently" that after one of the men got some wine, they all shared it "communion-like." Typical thing for a preacher to say—it seemed. There was no way to anticipate that the sermon would in fact conclude with the eucharistic image. On reflection, the men's sharing of the bottle becomes a pathetic substitute communion. Hardly an accident.

The preparation process for including such foreshadowing moments requires thinking in reverse, normally. Late in the sermon preparation process, after the key turns of the plot have been established, the preacher simply asks whether there is an earlier moment that can actually key the later major turn or event. What can be said that will create anticipation without "letting the cat out of the bag"? Such an insertion will further empower the effect of the crucial later moment.

Third, the *interior flashback*—a method of including past data without interrupting the present tense of the story line: Noah has just been discovered by Ham, and what was supposed to be the morning after is now clearly going to be the morning before. The gripping drama ought not be interrupted by reference to any point in Noah's past life, and yet the preacher senses that to best understand this moment, the past must somehow be made present. So Noah begins to pray and reminds God of the past. Of course, we are reminded too. Noah even reminds God of his painful-to-wear hat, which is just what the listeners need to know. And, of course, we cannot argue much—who can argue against someone's prayer? Notice how often memory is summoned in various kinds of narrative literature. Its purpose is to bring to the present scene something important from the past—yet without interrupting the present flow.

One may ask, Well, why not include the incident or aspect of the past before, when it actually happened? Willis certainly could have talked about the hat just after the storm ended. But it would have felt out of place there—not leading where the sermon was going. To delay the appearance of the hat until now gains the power of immediate juxtaposition.

This technique is one of the easiest to accomplish. When a sermon plot line (as you are preparing it) arrives at a decisive moment that has had its power sapped because too much story line has come between the present moment and a past moment of impacting potential, you simply have the character remember. The key is to *interrupt* the present moment with the remembering. For example, your sermonic character is asked a question. Don't allow the character to answer the question and then remember. The flashback occurs between the question and the answer. Again, the key is not to wait until a break in the action; interrupt something. Thus, the father is begging his older son to come into the welcome-home party for the prodigal. What does the older son do? He makes his father remember with "Lo, these many years . . . "

We need to observe here that the technique of an interior flashback is not the only way to accomplish immediate juxtaposition of events of different times. Another method is to formulate the plot line a totally different way. You will recall that we are presently discussing the narrative sermonic option called *running the story*. Another option is to suspend the story, which might involve an exterior flashback. For this latter option we will focus on another sermon altogether. But in order to anticipate that discussion, we can note that Willis could have started his Noah sermon with the tent scene and then suspended the action altogether in order to go back to the Flood. More about this option later. Here we should note what is accomplished with an interior flashback—namely, the opportunity to bring past events present without interrupting the present flow of the story line.

Reprise

This narrative technique is easier to describe than to name. The term *reprise*, coming from the musical world, suggests it but is not quite accurate because technically *reprise* means a return to the original theme. "Just one more time," the jazz leader calls out, just as the listeners think the number is over—and we're closer to what I have in mind here. What I *do* mean precisely is that often a sermon is not quite over when the narrative trip is complete. The preacher will back up—typically to the moment when the good news evoked the decisive homiletical turn—and do it again in some way. Then the preacher walks away with the remainder of the repeat *left unstated*. Willis shows us how.

The next to last sentence of the sermon appears to be the final one: "If he could get that far he could make a decision to turn his will and his life over to the care of a God who sees people through rainbows bright and colorful and pretty and made for creation." Surely the sermon is complete. Willis has already used the rainbow image to evoke the good news—the indicative of the gospel. Finally, he showed how life could be different as a result of Noah's getting in touch with that good news—the imperative of the gospel's claim. And we're done—but Willis isn't. He adds one more sentence: "Made to be fed by a God who cares so much that God transforms the Divine body into bread that we can eat and into a wine that anybody can drink."

At least three things are going on here. First, one of the central problems of any sermon, narrative or otherwise, is that it tends to remain behind the pulpit. Even the narrative sermon, with its increased capacity for congregational participation, often gains closure while still in the preacher's hands. But note what happens with the abbreviated "one more time" technique. When the good news is once again announced but the consequences are left unstated, the *listeners* have to finish the reprise! In short, the "tag" serves to put the ball in their court. Did you notice that in that last sentence, Willis did not say "he could," Willis said "we can"?

Second, since the good news has already been announced *and* connected to its consequences, a quick return allows the preacher to state it with powerful aesthetic imagery. The listeners already know the terms of closure, so nothing is left dangling; now they receive evocation.

Third, this technique results in the final sentence of the sermon being focused on divine action, not on human response. Listeners have grown accustomed to the preacher's continual and detailed concentration on what we need to do, ought to do, must do. By means of this reprise technique folks are left with what God has done. Good theology, seems to me.

In the case of the Noah sermon the final "tag" was only one sentence. This need not be the case. It may well be much longer than that, depending on the particularities of a given sermon. What *is* important is that it not be so long that listeners begin to wonder if the preacher forgot what had already been said. The language ought to be the most crisp and evocative of the entire sermon. When used with greatest power, the closing phrase is metaphorical, as was the case with Willis's Eucharist image. In this way people are left with the metaphoric tease.

Narrative Norms

Among the various narrative norms operative in the Noah sermon, several deserve our attention here.

Point of View

By this phrase I am presuming a broader definition than its technical usage in narrative theory literature. I am thinking about the ebb and flow of distance between the teller and the story, as well as the "placement" of the telling.

In order to consider this norm, imagine that you are taking your child for a ride on an excursion boat on a large river. You have your camera in hand in order to record this important event. Of course, you take her picture as she hands the ticket to the guide, and, naturally, a picture of the boat itself. One really fine snapshot shows her in the captain's hat, sitting at the bow of the ship with hills at the water's edge. One picture shows a piece of scenery that would not even reveal that you took it from a boat, except that the picture got blurred when the motion of the waves jostled you. Once, she borrows the camera to take your picture, and later a boat acquaintance takes a picture of the two of you together. After the ride is complete, you are impressed by some of the artifacts in the museum, and you take one shot of a picture that depicts the actual building of the boat. Finally, you get a panoramic snapshot of the entire scene—boat, museum, river, and hills. Meanwhile, the river continues to flow, and the power of the boat's engines continue to work it upstream, even though in the picture the boat appears to be standing still at the loading dock.

Notice that the pictures all reflect different distances of time and space from the facticity of the action itself. *Before, during, inside, about, from, at,* and *by* are all terms that refer to *different relations* between you and the boatride. Something similar is true between the preacher and the action of a biblical story.

"Noah was a good man"—the opening line—is an editorial comment by the preacher. "See Noah on the deck of a ship: the wind blows, the waters rise . . . ," and we are invited into the action, although we are still looking at it. "What do you do with a drunken sailor?" does not literally require Noah's presence at all. "We would sail with you anywhere" is another editorial comment actually made by another narrator, yet included by this one. "Oh,

God" happens from inside Noah himself. "He lifts the wine skin and, sweet Jesus, it's not empty" is a mix of two points at once, and "Mogan David" has a different setting altogether. So what might be the applicable rules in the telling of a story?

First of all, the power of this telling of the story centers on the close proximity of teller and action. Willis never tarried long with one foot in and the other out. Likewise, editorial comments of a more general sort are quite limited, a fact made possible because *how* he narrated the story allowed us to know his position without his slipping out to say so. Only once did he actually leave the story to tell another, and never did he speak of the fact of the story being included in the wider context of the canon of Scripture.

From all of this we might name several position points along the continuum called "Distance Between Teller and Story": (1) *inside* the character, (2) *inside* the story, (3) *about* the character, (4) *about* the story, and (5) *away* from the story. This, obviously, is a bit too simple (for example, it deals with only one character) and a bit too arbitrary, but I believe it allows us to at least visualize what we are considering.

Of course, it depends upon the story, the occasion, and other factors, but my experience is that biblical story–based sermons that manage a combination of positions two and three tend toward a happy blend of simplicity and power. Certainly, sermons that linger very long in positions one, four, or five tend to run into trouble for the following reasons.

When you move from "he said" to actual first-person portrayal (from position two to one, above)—that is, into dramatic characterization—you enter dangerous territory. Once the teller *becomes* the character, listeners tend to watch how well the preacher is "acting out the part" and hence begin to distance themselves in order to "watch." Note that Willis moved into characterization only during the brief prayer lines. With a different text one can easily imagine the following: "The father literally begged his son to come into the party, but to no avail. 'When did you ever throw a party for me?' 'Son, you know everything of mine is yours already.' But the son turned back to the barn." Notice how the incident begins in third person, moves into first person, stays there only briefly, and ends back in third person. The point is, most of us can believably sustain only brief moments of characterization.

Likewise, all of us have experienced the trap of staying inside the story (positions two and three), finishing the story, and then elaborating and elaborating topically on the moral conclusions to be drawn. At least when Willis moved away from the story (position five), he turned to another story, not to topical address. And he did it only once.

Now, having said all this about my preference for staying as close to the story line as possible, making few excursions into editorial comment and summary, the truth is, not all texts will allow such simplicity.

Some texts simply are too short to be sustained throughout an entire narrative sermon. Other texts are too complicated to be utilized without giving textual or contextual comment. Other texts run straight toward dead ends and need outside help of some kind, from the teller, from another text, or from a previous episode. Simply put, not all texts will work with the "run the story" sermonic design. This is why we will be discussing other options by means of other sermons. But before moving on, a question emerges: What do I do when, rather briefly, I must move to other material, exegetical or editorial? How do I make the necessary transitions without ruining the story line? Willis can help us here.

Transitions

We have already noted in the running commentary how Willis once interrupted Noah's next drink in order to use the Gatlin song illustration. He had uncorked the wineskin—even choked on its smell—but had not yet taken the drink. Naturally, it is easy for the preacher to get back. There are other transitions worth noting.

When moving from a farther to a closer position,

sometimes no transitional line is needed at all. So after "Noah was a good man," Willis simply continues, "See Noah on the deck." The problem more likely will be in making transitions from close to the action to farther away. Sometimes the use of a question rather than a statement is helpful. So when our preacher was finished with his brief look at Ham, he needed to find a way back to Noah. He asked a question, "What do you do . . . ?" as the means to traverse the territory.

Willis often would use a common ingredient to make a transition. For example, once he finished the Gatlin song illustration, he needed to get back to the drink that had been left just outside Noah's lips. To negotiate the transition, he closes the Gatlin illustration with "Will there be a balm in Gilead?" The next line begins "There is no balm for Noah." And since Willis knows we now remember that Noah is about to take a drink, he keeps us waiting—and notes how "one sip is too much and a thousand won't be enough" (really a generalization about alcoholism). Willis even adds another brief prayer, and *then* says, "And he lifts the wine skin . . . and he drinks."

Sometimes transitions from close distance to far are facilitated principally by choosing vital language instead of pale. When Willis wanted a momentary reference to the past, he could have said, "Previously in his life . . . " But he didn't. What he said was "There was a time when . . . "

The safest rule regarding successfully making such transitions is simply: leave with ambiguity, not closure, and then return by the same door. When you must leave close proximity to the action of the story line for a piece of exegesis, lead the story line to the point where the exegetical piece is required.

For example, you are preaching on the good Samaritan text and, having done your exegetical homework, realize that the moment when the Samaritan stopped to minister to the wounded man was a shocking moment, not simply because one of those Samaritans would offer assistance (we probably know that part), but because the Jewish man in the ditch *would not want* the help. Now, the lawyer and other Jewish listeners to the story understand that, but probably not the majority of today's congregation. You would be ill advised to preface the story with such exegetical data, not only because few would listen to such detail but also because the story would lose its power. Nor would you want to break the action just before the critical moment: "Now, we need to note here that this is a Samaritan, and you recall how they and the Jews felt about each other."

What you might do is build the anticipation of possible assistance with "But now he hears someone else coming. Maybe he will stop to help. But his hopes are dashed quickly, not because this person is going to pass by like the others, but because he is, indeed, *going to stop!*" The listeners, you hope, are shocked to hear this, momentarily confused until the preacher continues: "And in a moment's flash he remembers the saying: 'The Jew who accepts help from a Samaritan delays the coming of the kingdom.' He prays the Samaritan will pass by . . . but he doesn't." Such information, then, is presented when it becomes required and is given in some way that avoids interruption of the story line.

Variation of Narrative Movement

Any plot line must have variation of suspense or torque in order to keep the listeners from "jumping ship." It is not enough simply to be certain that suspense is built in. Perhaps you recall how, early in the sermon, Willis brings the ship safely in to shore. His choice of language, with its fluid images, helps us sense that the tension level decreases. But, of course, not for long. The momentary lessening of torque will soon be replaced by more torque yet. We have already observed in the running commentary how Willis slowed the pace in order for us to absorb the weight of meaning at several critical junctures in the story line.

Such variation is effected in numerous ways. Presentational vocal factors, such as pitch, rate, quality, and intonation, are included, of course. But effective narrative pacing is accomplished also by such variables as the weight and speed of cognitive meaning, the simplicity or complexity of word choice, the character of the syntax utilized, and the nature of the language itself. This whole matter of narrative movement can be sensed in the musical function of rhythm. My best advice regarding how to get in touch with this issue is for the preacher to imagine being an orchestra conductor and, with the arms, to literally direct the sermonic composition (in the study, of course, not in the pulpit).

Characterization

The credibility of the telling of a biblical story, it seems to me, centers in large measure on how well the preacher gets the listeners inside the principal character or characters. As long as we look *at* a character, we tend to remain in a kind of "we/they" polarity. Quickly we make judgments based on their behavior, which generally does not measure up to our standards of minimal virtue. Strange it is, however, what happens when we look *with* a character. All of a sudden we are in an "I-Thou" mode of being. In order to "look with" one must get inside a character. It is amazing how fluid things are in there, when compared to how set things are outside. It is the difference between observing behavior and understanding motives. Behavior is so "objective," whereas the possible motives are more "subjective"—you can't be sure. Often I will suggest to students that before they begin, sermonically, to condemn faulty behavior, they should imagine it being performed by a dear friend of theirs.

The intent here is not to find excuses for unchristian behavior, but to gain accuracy about causality. Moreover, such harder homiletical work will result in the narrativity keeping its motion instead of consisting of episodal chunks of concrete. For example, note the negative consequence for narrative openness or fluidity when, in the case of the woman taken in adultery, the preacher quickly concludes that the reason the rock-toting men wanted to stone the woman is that they were implicated in her behavior. The sermon screeches to a stop here. My hunch is that the preacher's eyes focused on the evil character of the moment, felt obliged to damn such behavior, and, hence, *then* sought a motive equal in evil to the behavior. Actually, the rock-toting men turn out to be the heroes of the story, with Jesus following their example and saying "neither do I."

The central focus of the Noah sermon is the drunken episode—hardly appropriate for a biblical hero. Repeatedly, Willis keeps the listeners inside the fluidity of motive.

So much for the observable capabilities of narrative form, the techniques utilized, and the narrative norms explicatable from "Noah Was a Good Man" by Dennis Willis. It is time now to experience another sermon that will feature another biblical narrative design altogether.

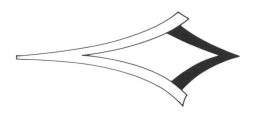

Delaying the Story

Sometimes running the story is not the best way to handle a text within a narrative sermon shape. As I suggested earlier, it may be wise to *delay* the story, beginning the sermon somewhere else. Such is the case with "Limited Resources; Unlimited Possibilities" by Dr. Leander E. Keck, Academic Dean at Yale Divinity School.

The context for the sermon surely is one of at least two major reasons he selected this method. This sermon was preached in the Chapel at Candler School of Theology when Dr. Keck was a professor of New Testament there. Clearly, Dr. Keck perceives a pastoral need within that seminary community of such moment that he decides to begin with that issue. Moreover, the text he has chosen provides the resolution to that pastoral need. You will notice that even the reading of the text is delayed until he is well inside the sermon. Once he has named the problem and allowed the issue to gain complication, he then moves to the text. Since he is a professor of New Testament, his not beginning with a text surely must have caught many listeners by surprise and served thus to further empower it once it is introduced.

Listen, then, for our preacher, Dr. Leander E. Keck, *delaying the story.*

(Please read out loud.)

"Limited Resources, Unlimited Possibilities"
by
Leander E. Keck

At one time or other, all of us have wondered, "Just what am I doing here?" I am not concerned just now with the bewilderment that is a symptom of an unclear vocation. I am concerned now with that gnawing, demoralizing sense of inadequacy which often seeps into the seminary community.

Indeed, the curriculum appears to be designed to rob a student of confidence. On the one hand, horizons are pushed back so that we are overwhelmed by the enormity of the problems we face. The simple pulpit answers for which the church is known are shown to be thin and short. Healing the gnarled and twisted human lives we touch takes far more than "a decision for Christ." Even the task of coming to terms with ourselves turns out to be overwhelming, the more we learn that we cannot run away from who we are and have become at the hands of parents, small-town expectations, or our own illusions. Besides, unsnarling the tangled threads of our society takes more than evangelistic crusades, more than marches, more even than hard-won victories in elections. The tension between the remedies for inflation and the remedies for depression stands for the baffling complexity of our world. Our situation is quite like that of the Israelite reconnaissance into Canaan in the time of Moses. You recall that the spies returned not simply with tales on their lips about the milk and honey, but also with terror in their hearts because there were giants in the land—giants so much in command of the situation that there seemed to be no point in pitting the puny resources of the Hebrews against them.

On the other hand, our feeling of adequacy is eroded by the seminary experience itself in another way—we find that we no longer believe what we once believed as firmly as we once believed it. Not only do we become more aware of what the gospel has to contend with, but late one night we might discover that we are no longer sure what the gospel is. All this critical analysis has gotten to us—a pretty good sign that the faculty is doing its job. Even if we learn about the past victories over persecuting caesars, it is not clear that we ourselves could take them on. We are not sure we can use our weapons. True, we have been taught how to disassemble our rifles and to name the parts—you know, J, E, D, P, Q, Proto-Luke, and Deutero-Paul. But now we have trouble getting it back together. Some of us are afraid that when we need it most, it will not work for us the way it used to; while others wonder whether there is any firepower at all in such a scripture as the Bible turns out to be.

This deep uneasiness and ambivalence would be more manageable if we could simply concentrate on sorting ourselves out, on finding that most precious commodity of all, identity. The quest for identity has become more important than it ought to be. This is because we are in a bewildered culture, set in the midst of a time and place where people are seeking something to hold onto, something that makes sense, something to count on. For the first time since we Europeans began pushing the Indians back from the shore, it is no longer clear that our children will fare better than we did. For the first time there rises up the spectre of our grandchildren calling us to account for having robbed them by our throw-away economy. It might not be long before my generation will be indicted for believing its own propaganda about the glories of the American way of life, blessed and sanctified by educators, politicians, and clergy. Where is the articulate and incisive person who can tell our people the truth in a way that will be heard? It is fairly easy to be shrill with the truth, but who can say it effectively so that new alternatives appear? Our churches are as uncertain as the culture they bless. What is more disheartening than the Saturday paper, laden with dilemmas and crises on one page, burdened with the church ads on the next—ads which boldly announce sermons and programs which appear to leave our people hungry and groping.

In other words, we are becoming aware of the world and aware of ourselves precisely at a time when we can no longer afford the luxury of finding ourselves above all. The very impulses that brought us here also set our faces toward this hunger for a word of truth or a deed which has integrity. It would be absurd to think that we are the only ones who are caught between massive needs and personal inadequacy, for teachers, social workers, and economists also are in this plight. But my concern is with us.

Our diagnosis has not been thorough, but it is enough to suggest that we need to hear a story. And strangely, it's a story whose point a prosaic mind can miss. In fact, on one level it's completely unbelievable; on another level, it can . . . but why spoil the story in advance?

The apostles returned to Jesus, and told him all that they had done and taught. And he said to them, "Come away by yourselves to a lonely place, and rest a while." For many were coming and going, and they had no leisure even to eat. And they went away in the boat to a lonely place by themselves. Now many saw them going, and knew them, and they ran there on foot from all the towns, and got there ahead of them. As he went ashore he saw a great throng, and he had compassion on them, because they were like sheep without a shepherd; and he began to teach them many things. And when it grew late, his disciples came to him and said, "This is a lonely place, and the hour is now late; send them away, to go into the country and villages round about and buy themselves something to eat." But he answered them, "You give them something to eat." And they said to him, "Shall we go and buy two hundred denarii worth of bread, and give it to them to eat?" And he said to them, "How many loaves have you? Go and see." And when they had

found out, they said, "Five, and two fish." Then he
commanded them all to sit down by companies upon the
green grass. So they sat down in groups, by hundreds and
by fifties. And taking the five loaves and the two fish he
looked up to heaven, and blessed, and broke the loaves,
and gave them to the disciples to set before the people;
and he divided the two fish among them all. And they all
ate and were satisfied. And they took up twelve baskets
full of broken pieces and of the fish. And those who ate
the loaves were five thousand men. (Mark 6:30-44)

That story illumines where we find ourselves, and what
we may expect. It might not be easy to get with the beat of
this story. We have labeled it the story of the Multiplication
of the Loaves and Fishes, and tourist guides in the Holy
Land will take you to the ruins of a church built on the
exact place where it happened. But Mark is not as
interested in the miraculous as we are; in fact he doesn't
tell us what happened to the bread and fish. He does tell us
what happened to people. But back to the story.

Here is a crowd of people, thronging around Jesus. To
him, they suggested sheep without a shepherd, milling
about. Have you ever seen shepherdless sheep? We must
not think of a dozen sheep fenced in the south 40 of a
north Georgia farm. We ought to see bands of sheep in
the far West. These herds are wholly dependent on the
shepherd for pasture and protection. Take away the
shepherd and his dog, and they simply wander around,
nibbling their way into danger and death, baa-baaing
their fears into the night. Despite our city ways, we have
enough imagination left to see that the image is that of
our culture with no leadership worth naming, and no
truth to feed on. And now it's time to eat.

The disciples were sensitive to the situation and to the
needs of persons. They also know where they are—out
among the hills and gulleys of Palestine. So they suggest,
"This is a lonely place and the hour is now late. Send
them away to go into the countryside and villages round

about and buy themselves something to eat." What could better combine compassion with realism? They clearly believe in responsible social action based on the contextual ethic.

But Jesus has something else in mind. To such a practical suggestion he responds with something quite ridiculous: "You give them something to eat." The disciples are flabbergasted. So they explode with frustration, "Shall we go and buy 200 denarii worth of bread and give it to them to eat?" That's about eight months' pay. Where are they to get that kind of money just now? No credit card could bail them out.

This is where we find ourselves, is it not? Overwhelmed by need before us and overwhelmed by inadequacy within ourselves, we nonetheless hear this command, "You give them something to eat." And so like our predecessors, we protest that too much is expected of us. "Shall we go somewhere to get supplies?" To paraphrase, Shall we go to Emory, to graduate school—at least get a D.Min.? Shall we collect supplies from Tillich, or Moltmann, or Ruether? Shall we go to the conservatives, whose churches are growing, or to the charismatics?

But Jesus does not send them anywhere to get supplies. He asks a question so simple and so irrelevant that they wonder whether he is in touch with reality. "How many loaves have you? Go see." What difference does it make how many loaves they had? It wouldn't be enough to feed this crowd. But nonetheless, they go look; perhaps they hope to scrounge up a little anyway. When they return, their report sounds like Mother Hubbard on food stamps: "Sir, we have five loaves and two fish." Things are worse than they thought. That's not even enough for Jesus, and the disciples, not even half a loaf apiece, and those fish weren't twenty-pound salmon either.

Surely Jesus will get back to reality now and dismiss the crowd. There's nothing to be done with such resources. We have no trouble identifying with the disciples. We too stand there with our five sandwiches and two sardines, facing a needy world. It's that old story again: the spies and the giants, David and Goliath, Paul in Ephesus, Schweitzer in Lambarene, Martin Luther King in Montgomery, you and I in Atlanta. But we cannot ignore the world in order to divide what we have among ourselves, cozy and "fellowshippy" though it would be. Jesus is not stymied. He orders the crowd to sit in groups of fifties and hundreds. And now he takes those loaves and fish and says the blessing and divides them just as any Jewish father would do at home. Then he gives the bread to the disciples to distribute. Can you image their embarrassment as they stood in line, waiting for their turn to get the bread, knowing that ten thousand eyes were watching and five thousand stomachs growling?

Now our curiosity is strained. We want to know how Jesus did it. But curiosity goes hungry while the crowd is fed. Mark wants us to see the people, not the loaves. The crowd had more than enough to eat, and there were twelve baskets of leftovers. And don't ask where they got the baskets either!

Mark's picture is coming through now. The crowd is fed when Jesus takes the meager resources and gives his blessing. That's the word of God even for seminarians. Persons can be fed even through our piddling resources. They will be fed not because the loaves and fish belong to us, nor because they are special loaves, but simply because things happen that way when our resources are put at the disposal of Jesus. This would be just as true if we had one loaf and one fish for every man, woman, and child.

If we cannot see this clearly enough on the Synoptic network, we can turn to Paul's: Corinthians, channel 2. The Corinthians do not know what to make of Paul. Paul tells them that they do not understand his role because they do not understand the gospel. They think that the apostle's effectiveness is to be measured by his rhetoric, by his philosophical gyrations, by the power of his ecstatic experiences. When measured by this yardstick, the apostle doesn't come off so well. He has only five loaves and two fish, and there are many sophisticated Corinthians to be fed. They want a preacher about whose prowess they can boast.

Well, says Paul, I can boast too. Listen to his boasting: "Five times I have received at the hands of the Jews the forty lashes less one. Three times I have been beaten with rods; once I was stoned. Three times I have been shipwrecked; a night and a day . . . adrift at sea; on frequent journeys, in danger from rivers, danger from robbers, danger from my own people, danger from Gentiles, danger in the city, danger in the wilderness. . . . And apart from other things, there is the daily pressure upon me of my anxiety for all the churches." What kind of boasting is that? It is boasting about having only five loaves and two fish, or as Paul puts it, "If I must boast, I will boast of the things that show my weakness."

And if this public record has not revealed how weak he is, his private inner life does. So he tells of his religious experience, that element so greatly prized in Corinth— and in Georgia. He was caught up to the third heaven, where he heard wondrous things. Surely this ought to get him beyond the five measly loaves. But now listen as Paul continues: "To keep me from being too elated by the abundance of revelations, a thorn was given me in the flesh, . . . to keep me from being too elated. Three times I besought the Lord about this, that it should leave me; but he said to me, "My grace is sufficient for you, for my power is made perfect in weakness.' "

There you have it. The same Lord who did not get nervous when he looked down at the little lunch said to Paul, "My power is made perfect in your five loaves." And Paul managed to lay hold of enough grace to say, "I will all the more gladly boast of my weaknesses, that the power of Christ may rest upon me. For the sake of Christ, then, I am content with weaknesses, insults, hardships, persecutions, and calamities; for when I am weak, then I am strong." Paul says this because Christ has blessed him in his weakness, has shown how the power of the gospel is not the same as the strength of the apostle. Mark would have said it this way, "When the disciples have only five loaves and two fish they have plenty because Christ will make it more than enough." I can put it this way: "When I face the world with my limited resources I need not panic because Christ can make them adequate by blessing them."

I recall preaching a sermon so weak that I wished I could have sneaked out the back way. But at the door, a person who seldom commented made it a point to say that the sermon had been helpful. To this day I can't see what it could have been that helped her, but one of my little loaves was blessed and she was fed.

I also recall an incident when I was in the Boston City Hospital taking my clinical training. One day the chaplain called on a patient who had been visited by one of us. The patient said the visit was almost as if God himself had entered his room. The chaplain was eager to find out who made this tremendous call and to read his verbatim report. He found out that the student who made the call didn't bother to write it up because he had no idea that he had been the vehicle for the divine presence, and that his loaf had been blessed enough for a lonely patient to be fed.

All sorts of things happen when our five loaves are put to work. Fifteen years ago, a group of students had only five loaves of determination to be treated equally, and sat in at a lunch counter, and began a revolution. Who knows what you and I might yet be called upon to do or say?

To such a list of experiences you yourself may add—if you risk using your five loaves to feed the crowd. And then this story will come true again, for the point is not what happened to the bread but what happened to the people when the bread was blessed. Generation after generation has been fed by weak disciples serving their own five loaves with Christ's blessing. This is the real apostolic succession, and now it's our turn. You give them something to eat.

A more classic example of *delaying the story* cannot be imagined. It fits exactly the narrative sermonic model. Again, it is time for the homiletical exegesis or running commentary, after which we will consider several narrative features.

Running Commentary

At one time or other, all of us have wondered, "Just what am I doing here?" I am not concerned just now with the bewilderment that is a symptom of an unclear vocation. I am concerned now with that gnawing, demoralizing sense of inadequacy which often seeps into the seminary community.

Leander Keck begins the sermon with an opening conflict. Three aspects of it ought to be noted: First, the conflict is theirs, not his. He begins with the listeners' world. Second, he clarifies the conflict, lest listeners be misled into another one. Third, there is no biblical text evident. And this is a professor of New Testament, preaching in chapel. Surprise.

Indeed, the curriculum appears to be designed to rob a student of confidence. On the one hand, horizons are pushed back so that we are overwhelmed by the enormity of the problems we face. The simple pulpit answers for which the church is known are shown to be thin and short. Healing the gnarled and twisted human lives we touch takes far more than "a decision for Christ." Even the task of coming to terms with ourselves turns out to be overwhelming, the more we learn that we cannot run away from who we are and have become at the hands of parents, small-town expectations, or our own illusions. Besides, unsnarling the tangled threads of our society takes more than evangelistic crusades, more than marches, more even than hard-won victories in elections. The tension between the remedies for inflation and the remedies for depression stands for the baffling complexity of our world. Our situation is quite like that of

*the Israelite reconnaissance into Canaan in the time of
Moses. You recall that the spies returned not simply with
tales on their lips about the milk and honey, but also with
terror in their hearts because there were giants in the
land—giants so much in command of the situation that
there seemed to be no point in pitting the puny resources
of the Hebrews against them.*

Immediately, the opening conflict becomes complicated. Note that he catches the listeners at both ends of the
dilemma. On the one hand, the curriculum robs us of
confidence because it exposes the enormous range of the
world's need. At the same time it increases the demand for
adequacy, it robs us of what adequacy we thought we had.
But these two problems are not enough. Keck catches the
listeners in between these two extremes by observing that
we personally are caught by the exigencies of our
academic situations, quite apart from the rest. This
situation is not simply personally existential; it is formed
in the context of a baffling social context, and hence a
fourth complicating factor is introduced. All this, and we
are scarcely into the second minute of the sermon.

We should observe, also, how Keck has for the second
time made sure that the listeners are not going to go off on
a tangent. Lest some listeners bring quick closure to the
problem by blaming the seminary for causing the
problem, the preacher states without equivocation that the
pulpit we know provides thin answers.

Still we have no text, and the students' normal
expectations have to be causing further escalation of the
sense of suspense. Finally a biblical reference is utilized,
and some probably think it will be the formative biblical
base. Whatever it is, it serves now to make things even
worse. No doubt the preacher knows the term "terror"
will nicely summarize the listeners' sense of self—a sense
perhaps half forgotten until the sermon began.

*On the other hand, our feeling of adequacy is eroded
by the seminary experience itself in another way—we*

find that we no longer believe what we once believed as firmly as we once believed it. Not only do we become more aware of what the gospel has to contend with, but late one night we might discover that we are no longer sure what the gospel is. All this critical analysis has gotten to us—a pretty good sign that the faculty is doing its job. Even if we learn about the past victories over persecuting caesars, it is not clear that we ourselves could take them on. We are not sure we can use our weapons. True, we have been taught how to disassemble our rifles and to name the parts—you know, J, E, D, P, Q, Proto-Luke, and Deutero-Paul. But now we have trouble getting it back together. Some of us are afraid that when we need it most, it will not work for us the way it used to; while others wonder whether there is any firepower at all in such a scripture as the Bible turns out to be.

Indeed, now the bottom drops out altogether. We are forced to admit that we just may have been undone by our academic work and now are not even sure "what the gospel is." Note that Keck places that awful realization not as happening during the day but as happening "late one night." Our preacher does understand the metaphoric use of language.

Keck turns to analogy, and its choice is important to note. The use of any analogy carries with it both the potential of facilitating a powerful image and also the possibility of inadvertently detouring the movement of thought. Observe that the rifle imagery is essentially a positive one. The listeners surely cannot doubt that rifles can be counted on to work. Keck makes a clean and positive statement about the tools of biblical scholarship. Their utility is not to be questioned. The problem is not with the weapon; it is with our inability properly to make it useful. Well, there may be a few who wonder about it. And hence the preacher is able to maintain contact with various kinds of listeners. Without this partial sentence, Keck may be without some of his listeners. He senses this—and acts.

This deep uneasiness and ambivalence would be more manageable if we could simply concentrate on sorting ourselves out, on finding that most precious commodity of all, identity. The quest for identity has become more important than it ought to be. This is because we are in a bewildered culture, set in the midst of a time and place where people are seeking something to hold onto, something that makes sense, something to count on. For the first time since we Europeans began pushing the Indians back from the shore, it is no longer clear that our children will fare better than we did. For the first time there rises up the spectre of our grandchildren calling us to account for having robbed them by our throw-away economy. It might not be long before my generation will be indicted for believing its own propaganda about the glories of the American way of life, blessed and sanctified by educators, politicians, and clergy. Where is the articulate and incisive person who can tell our people the truth in a way that will be heard? It is fairly easy to be shrill with the truth, but who can say it effectively so that new alternatives appear? Our churches are as uncertain as the culture they bless. What is more disheartening than the Saturday paper, laden with dilemmas and crises on one page, burdened with the church ads on the next—ads which boldly announce sermons and programs which appear to leave our people hungry and groping.

Having set the scope and depth of the problem, Keck moves toward some solution—but note that the first solution considered will not suffice. At this point, one has to be impressed with how the preacher anticipates the possible responses to his message. He sniffs out what is a likely solution that some listeners are going to bring at this point. And, of course, he can be sure that they are ready. No preacher can name a problem this precisely and show such ramifications without knowing that listeners cannot, will not, tolerate such dis-ease. The need for closure is great, and we will grope for any way out of the dilemma.

Keck believes that "identity" might be the route about to be taken by the listeners, and he cuts them off at the pass.

He takes to task American history, contemporary economics, current political propaganda, and even the life of the church. All of this serves to discount one possible answer to the issue at hand.

In other words, we are becoming aware of the world and aware of ourselves precisely at a time when we can no longer afford the luxury of finding ourselves above all. The very impulses that brought us here also set our faces toward this hunger for a word of truth or a deed which has integrity. It would be absurd to think that we are the only ones who are caught between massive needs and personal inadequacy, for teachers, social workers, and economists also are in this plight. But my concern is with us.

So, Keck summarizes the problem. Two important results occur when the preacher summarizes in this fashion. First, it objectifies the problem, puts it "out there" at arm's length from the listeners' existential involvement. This appears to result in a reduction of sermonic torque. In the long run it actually does the reverse. Recall that Keck has put a number of faces on the problem, with the result that if he does not now compress the matter, it will lack handleable focus and become diffuse. Second, this crisp naming of the problem readies the listeners for a transition toward some kind of solution.

Our diagnosis has not been thorough, but it is enough to suggest that we need to hear a story. And strangely, it's a story whose point a prosaic mind can miss. In fact, on one level it's completely unbelievable; on another level, it can . . . but why spoil the story in advance?

Surely with great relief the listeners learn that in order to find a solution, a story is in order. Our New Testament professor finally will provide a biblical answer. We have been waiting patiently. But instead he tells us that the story will not provide an answer at all because, in fact, it is "unbelievable."

[Mark 6:30-44]

That story illumines where we find ourselves, and what we may expect. It might not be easy to get with the beat of this story. We have labeled it is story of the Multiplication of the Loaves and Fishes, and tourist guides in the Holy Land will take you to the ruins of a church built on the exact place where it happened. But Mark is not as interested in the miraculous as we are; in fact he doesn't tell us what happened to the bread and fish. He does tell us what happened to people. But back to the story.

The preacher is more than a fine biblical scholar here; he is a fine judge of listening behavior. Once again he senses that without direction the listeners immediately will begin pondering on the issue of the miraculous. If we do, we will take a detour away from the preacher's purpose. We need to note an important homiletical fact of life here, which is that the longer a listener concentrates on ingredients that will detour the sermonic process, the harder it will be for the preacher to reestablish the plot line. Hence, quickly Keck moves our attention from the miraculous to people.

Here is a crowd of people, thronging around Jesus. To him, they suggested sheep without a shepherd, milling about. Have you ever seen shepherdless sheep? We must not think of a dozen sheep fenced in the south 40 of a north Georgia farm. We ought to see bands of sheep in the far West. These herds are wholly dependent on the shepherd for pasture and protection. Take away the shepherd and his dog, and they simply wander around, nibbling their way into danger and death, baa-baaing their fears into the night. Despite our city ways, we have enough imagination left to see that the image is that of our culture with no leadership worth naming, and no truth to feed on. And now it's time to eat.

Note again that had Keck not set the stage for the problematic nature of this biblical story, we would not have the patience really to enter. People simply must have adequate reason to become involved in the detail of a story. If the story were introduced as the solution, the listeners would demand a quick rendering of the proposed answer. Instead, the preacher invites us, first, to find out why the story is unbelievable. In the process, of course, the solution is being prepared. So we are dropped into the middle of the action of the biblical story.

Observe too that the preacher has confidence that the cultural distance between then and now does not necessarily sap the power of the image. Indeed, I believe it is possible that often the imagination actually is whetted by the lack of familiarity.

The disciples were sensitive to the situation and to the needs of persons. They also know where they are—out among the hills and gulleys of Palestine. So they suggest, "This is a lonely place and the hour is now late. Send them away to go into the countryside and villages round about and buy themselves something to eat." What could better combine compassion with realism? They clearly believe in responsible social action based on the contextual ethic.

Keck avoids that pedantic form of connection making preachers often use with the overheard words "We are a lot like that . . . " or "They, like us . . . " He trusts us with an implicit connection. But one might ask, Suppose people don't make the connection? Any preacher knows the issue here—whether to presume lack of listener ability and hence insult the perceptive folks, or presume the reverse and lose the less perceptive. The answer is to presume the best and then later add a piece that will bring others on board, which is precisely what he does with the contemporary phrase about "responsible social action."

But Jesus has something else in mind. To such a practical suggestion he responds with something quite ridiculous: "You give them something to eat." The disciples are flabbergasted. So they explode with

frustration, "Shall we go and buy 200 denarii worth of
bread and give it to them to eat?" That's about eight
months' pay. Where are they to get that kind of money
just now? No credit card could bail them out.

Here Keck teaches us an important lesson about biblical
preaching and listener engagement. Note how he takes
the side of the disciples as opposed to the plan of Jesus.
Now, everybody knows that Jesus is correct and the
disciples must be wrong. But to say so now would be to
take the torque out of the tale. So, temporarily, the
disciples' ideas amount to a "practical suggestion," while
Jesus' plan is "ridiculous."

*This is where we find ourselves, is it not? Over-
whelmed by need before us and overwhelmed by
inadequacy within ourselves, we nonetheless hear this
command, "You give them something to eat." And so
like our predecessors, we protest that too much is
expected of us. "Shall we go somewhere to get
supplies?" To paraphrase, Shall we go to Emory, to
graduate school—at least get a D.Min.? Shall we collect
supplies from Tillich, or Moltmann, or Reuther? Shall we
go to the conservatives, whose churches are growing, or
to the charismatics?*

In order to enflesh the ramification of this moment in the
story, Keck now makes a direct reference to the listeners.
But it is not at all a pale "We are a lot like that" kind of
statement. Instead, he once more heightens the sense of
our dilemma. "Overwhelmed by inadequacy" we are,
while confronted by the command to do something.

He picks up our quest for greater knowledge, resources,
and skills and places them inside the biblical dialogue.
Note that when he does so he does not misrepresent the
text. He takes responsibility for it by saying, "To
paraphrase . . . "

*But Jesus does not send them anywhere to get supplies.
He asks a question so simple and so irrelevant that they
wonder whether he is in touch with reality. "How many*

loaves have you? Go see." What difference does it make how many loaves they had? It wouldn't be enough to feed this crowd. But nonetheless, they go look; perhaps they hope to scrounge up a little anyway. When they return, their report sounds like Mother Hubbard on food stamps: "Sir, we have five loaves and two fish." Things are worse than they thought. That's not even enough for Jesus, and the disciples, not even half a loaf apiece, and those fish weren't twenty-pound salmon either.

But, of course, there is nowhere else to turn. Again, Keck grants us permission to question the wisdom of Jesus, even to ask if "he is in touch with reality." In spite of the futility, they follow orders, and by saying so, Keck builds the tension.

When a story is well told, as in this case, those of us who would learn the art may not notice something very important here, which is that once you have begun a quickly moving paraphrase of a story that is about to lead to a decisive moment, you cannot turn back or lose courage. It is much like a jazz artist in the midst of a variation on a theme, who does not have the choice simply to play the original melody line through the last eight bars. Once in the middle, you stay in the mode until the end of the chorus.

Surely Jesus will get back to reality now and dismiss the crowd. There's nothing to be done with such resources. We have no trouble identifying with the disciples. We too stand there with our five sandwiches and two sardines, facing a needy world. It's that old story again: the spies and the giants, David and Goliath, Paul in Ephesus, Schweitzer in Lambarene, Martin Luther King in Montgomery, you and I in Atlanta. But we cannot ignore the world in order to divide what we have among ourselves, cozy and "fellowshippy" though it would be.

So now, as we arrive at the high point of the problem, established first in the context of the listeners' experience and now re-presented in the context of the biblical story, note how the preacher allows us company in our dilemma. Keck gives us heroes for this moment of truth. We are not alone but rather joined by a company of saints—all of us, caught in the impossible dilemma of the enormous needs of the world and our own inadequate resources. Note the connection between these lines and the title of the sermon.

Jesus is not stymied. He orders the crowd to sit in groups of fifties and hundreds. And now he takes those loaves and fish and says the blessing and divides them just as any Jewish father would do at home. Then he gives the bread to the disciples to distribute. Can you image their embarrassment as they stood in line, waiting for their turn to get the bread, knowing that ten thousand eyes were watching and five thousand stomachs growling?

Did you observe how unobstrusively Keck gives us a bit of biblical contextual information? He simply fits it in the sweep of a piece of action. Observe too that our preacher does not portray the moment in general terms, such as "and Jesus fed all the people." He gives us both visual and auditory images.

More important, he doesn't actually say the crowd was fed. He knows we will say that to ourselves. But in the next paragraph it will be assumed, as he asks, "How?"

Now our curiosity is strained. We want to know how Jesus did it. But curiosity goes hungry while the crowd is fed. Mark wants us to see the people, not the loaves. The crowd had more than enough to eat, and there were twelve baskets of leftovers. And don't ask where they got the baskets either!

Once again Keck is faced with the same old question he knows we will wonder about—the question about miracle. Again, he doesn't want us to go on a detour. Boldly he even adds a new ingredient we should have thought of in our temptation to turn aside from where the story is headed. He utilizes the story's own imagery in noting that "curiosity goes hungry."

Mark's picture is coming through now. The crowd is fed when Jesus takes the meager resources and gives his blessing. That's the word of God even for seminarians. Persons can be fed even through our piddling resources. They will be fed not because the loaves and fish belong to us, nor because they are special loaves, but simply because things happen that way when our resources are put at the disposal of Jesus. This would be just as true if we had one loaf and one fish for every man, woman, and child.

Now Keck is able to step away from the story itself for reflection upon this moment of good news. He had been inside the story line. Now he stands one step to the side, with one eye on the story and one eye on the listeners. And he highlights this crucial "aha" moment by calling it the "Word of God."

We need time to absorb the power of this redemptive moment of the good news. Keck uses it for reinforcement. Notice how the key idea of Jesus' transformation of our "piddling resources" is stated in three slightly different ways. He knew what to do with the time we needed.

If we cannot see this clearly enough on the Synoptic network, we can turn to Paul's: Corinthians, channel 2. The Corinthians do not know what to make of Paul. Paul tells them that they do not understand his role because they do not understand the gospel. They think that the apostle's effectiveness is to be measured by his rhetoric, by his philosophical gyrations, by the power of his ecstatic experiences. When measured by this yardstick, the apostle doesn't come off so well. He has only five loaves and two fish, and there are many sophisticated Corinthians to be fed. They want a preacher about whose prowess they can boast.

Well, says Paul, I can boast too. Listen to his boasting: "Five times I have received at the hands of the Jews the forty lashes less one. Three times I have been beaten with rods; once I was stoned. Three times I have been shipwrecked; a night and a day . . . adrift at sea; on frequent journeys, in danger from rivers, danger from robbers, danger from my own people, danger from Gentiles, danger in the city, danger in the wilderness. . . . And apart from other things, there is the daily pressure upon me of my anxiety for all the churches." What kind of boasting is that? It is boasting about having only five loaves and two fish, or as Paul puts it, "If I must boast, I will boast of the things that show my weakness."

Now our preacher is faced with a fairly momentous decision. The sermon has now made its decisive turn, and we are headed for home. What appears to remain, homiletically, is for the preacher to identify the consequences of this receipt of the good news. We will be shown how to appropriate this transforming power of Jesus, and indeed, we will be given the imperative to do so. The expectation of this final "chapter" of the sermon is clearly understood by preacher and listeners alike.

But Keck does not follow this expected plan. Instead, he moves to another figure, Paul, and to two more concrete issues. It is going to take almost three minutes to include this portion of the sermon. Should he do it?

Frankly, if he were the usual preacher in terms of preaching capacity, I would not recommend it, for the important reason that there is now the sense of release from a quite high level of tension. For the listeners to stay hooked to the sermon's new direction now requires a major decision on their part. This is particularly true when by means of detail it becomes evident that this is not going to be a brief aside but rather a significant consideration of the life of Paul.

Keck probably got away with the inclusion of this section on Paul—and for a very good reason. He already has the trust of the listeners. Not only do his listeners bring to this decisive moment their past experiences with him, but he has also already evidenced trustworthiness by how he has handled the sermon thus far. My hunch is that Keck knew the risks he was taking here and decided that the section drawn from Paul was necessary in order to accomplish his homiletical task. Obviously, there must be a good reason for this return to the original problem. Let's see what it is.

And if this public record has not revealed how weak he is, his private inner life does. So he tells of his religious experience, that element so greatly prized in Corinth—and in Georgia. He was caught up to the third heaven, where he heard wondrous things. Surely this ought to get him beyond the five measly loaves. But now listen as Paul continues: "To keep me from being too elated by the abundance of revelations, a thorn was given me in the flesh, . . . to keep me from being too elated. Three times I besought the Lord about this, that it should leave me; but he said to me, 'My grace is sufficient for you, for my power is made perfect in weakness.' "

It is not difficult to discern the reason for our preacher's excursion. Of all the biblical characters one can recall, none made so much about weakness as did Paul. It is difficult even to think of the apostle without remembering this component.

So when one is preaching on the subject of our own perceived inadequacies, how could Paul be excluded? Moreover, the matter is made richer in that it is not just our own perceived understanding here but now the expectations of those counting on our adequacy in ministry. Paul and the Corinthian church are perfect for the theme of this sermon. Once the listeners get the drift of this significance, their attention becomes inevitable.

There you have it. The same Lord who did not get nervous when he looked down at the little lunch said to Paul, "My power is made perfect in your five loaves." And Paul managed to lay hold of enough grace to say, "I will all the more gladly boast of my weaknesses, that the power of Christ may rest upon me. For the sake of Christ, then, I am content with weaknesses, insults, hardships, persecutions, and calamities; for when I am weak, then I am strong." Paul says this because Christ has blessed him in his weakness, has shown how the power of the gospel is not the same as the strength of the apostle. Mark would have said it this way, "When the disciples have only five loaves and two fish they have plenty because Christ will make it more than enough." I can put it this way: "When I face the world with my limited resources I need not panic because Christ can make them adequate by blessing them."

What is particularly impressive about Keck's inclusion of Paul in the sermon is the manner in which he blends the two accounts. This he accomplishes by means of the image of fish and loaves. Five times he either refers to or has Paul refer to his "measly loaves." This repeated use of the image does more than keep the sermon unified. It tells us, the listeners, that the Synoptic story is no fluke—indeed, cannot be dismissed as a strange account of a miracle. This is the same Lord, the same transforming power, that has been constant throughout the biblical record and the history of the church.

Moreover, by the time Paul—through Keck—gets through with us, weakness is no longer simply a limitation to be confessed but the key to our faithful service. Our weakness now becomes the doorway for the perfecting of Christ's power. What a reversal!

I recall preaching a sermon so weak that I wished I could have sneaked out the back way. But at the door, a person who seldom commented made it a point to say that the sermon had been helpful. To this day I can't see what it could have been that helped her, but one of my little loaves was blessed and she was fed.

All that is needed now is a brief imaging of how it works. Note that Keck does not apply this word to us first but to himself. And he does it without bragging: "To this day I can't see . . . " The Synoptic loaf that he placed in Paul's hand he now puts in his own. The redemptive action is Christ's, not the preacher's.

I also recall an incident when I was in the Boston City Hospital taking my clinical training. One day the chaplain called on a patient who had been visited by one of us. The patient said the visit was almost as if God himself had entered his room. The chaplain was eager to find out who made this tremendous call and to read his verbatim report. He found out that the student who made the call didn't bother to write it up because he had no idea that he had been the vehicle for the divine presence, and that his loaf had been blessed enough for a lonely patient to be fed.

Keck adds a second incident for good measure. He doesn't tell us who the student was whose call had such powerful effect. It might have been Keck himself, but if so he didn't tell us, and for good reason. The preacher can never be the source of the redemptive power of a sermon illustration. This temptation to share with parishioners just how helpful our ministry is had become so self-serving in the recent past that when I took preaching courses in seminary, the professor insisted that we never say anything about ourselves in a sermon. Seems to me this cure is a bit radical, particularly if you believe that preaching has to do with truth through personality. But we all know the problem. Keck avoids it.

All sorts of things happen when our five loaves are put to work. Fifteen years ago, a group of students had only five loaves of determination to be treated equally, and sat in at a lunch counter, and began a revolution. Who knows what you and I might yet be called upon to do or say?

Now our preacher turns the focus toward the listeners and their lives. Yet note the inclusiveness. Keck did not say "your"; he said "our." With apparent pride Keck focuses upon the crucial ministry of previous students—predecessors to the bulk of the congregation. Keck makes of it a challenge to us.

To such a list of experiences you yourself may add—if

you risk using your five loaves to feed the crowd. And then this story will come true again, for the point is not what happened to the bread but what happened to the people when the bread was blessed. Generation after generation has been fed by weak disciples serving their own five loaves with Christ's blessing. This is the real apostolic succession, and now it's our turn. You give them something to eat.

Hence, it is time now to anticipate the future, made new by the evocative power of this expression of the Word. We should observe how Keck now places matters in the listeners' hands. He announces that "this story *will* come true," not must or ought. It *will* come true because the bread will be blessed. There's no moralism here; this is description. Not "you must" but "you can." He places the ball in everybody's court by saying, "And now it's our turn." And his final sentence—the concluding word—returns us back inside the biblical story itself. It is not Keck's word at all. It is Christ's.

Narrative Capabilities, Techniques, and Norms

Once again, it will be helpful to highlight several features that emerge from our experience of the sermon. As before, we will consider narrative capabilities, narrative techniques, and narrative norms. We will name only some of the variables that are prompted by Keck's sermon.

Narrative Capabilities

Enhancement of the Relationship of Preacher to Text and Preacher to Listeners

Both the narrative form a sermon takes and the use of a central biblical story help create a quite different relational genre between preacher and text. The narrative form encourages a probing, inductive exploration of any text. The preacher is seen more as a seeker for and less as an explainer of the text. It is *less authoritarian* in the sense of the preacher being the expert, and *more authoritative* in the sense of the text's dominance in the experience. The preacher is more likely to be placed in the servant role.

Ironically, at the same time the presence of the preacher is more obvious. There is no place to hide; the sheer fact of the preacher's interpretative role is up front. There is less opportunity for "objective" assertions without the listeners' noticing the preacher's role in the process. Let me illustrate.

When Keck notes that with this text from Mark "it might not be easy to get with the beat of this story," he immediately names the crucial distinction between text and any reader or listener. Note that he then goes on to say *not* that Mark is not particularly interested in the miraculous but that "Mark is not *as* interested as we are." What is going on here is far more important than the subject matter at hand, the miraculous; what is going on here is a critical statement of *placement*, which puts Keck *in with the listeners, not in with the text*. Later he observes our "curiosity" about the scriptural scene, with the same result. The very nature of narrative movement from opening conflict to final denouement elicits this searching kind of placement. How different it is from the kind of biblical exposition of a text I grew accustomed to hearing at an early age. In that case the pronouncement of the text was explained to us and elaborated on. The preacher's identification vis-á-vis the text had much more to do with an implicit harmony between the preacher's word and the biblical truth. The fact that the preacher was an interpreter was seldom named or made obvious. The preacher knew what it meant, and soon we would too.

Moreover, the handling of a biblical text that is itself in narrative form—that is, a story—underscores the matter further. Just to reenact or to paraphrase and elaborate the details of a biblical story makes explicit the interpretative role of the preacher. When through the disciples' behavior

Keck wonders out loud about the question of Jesus' "being in touch with reality," the listeners are made keenly aware of the preacher's presence. It also makes the preacher vulnerable.

Being seen so clearly as interpreter leaves the preacher susceptible to censure as well as praise. Recall that Keck does not say simply that the disciples thought Jesus' response "something ridiculous," Keck calls it ridiculous. It's always possible that some listener may find that statement offensive. Rather than being a result to be avoided, such a possible reaction is precisely the desired position of vulnerability that enhances the potential power of a sermon. Simply put, trust of the preacher is central to faithful and effective preaching of the Word. Without vulnerability, trust remains shallow.

In short, I believe that narrative form and the use of a biblical story within that narrative form enhance the kind of relationship to text and to congregation that the preacher needs for powerful preaching.

Overcoming Cultural Distance

I hear numerous preachers wonder whether the great gulf of culture between biblical times and our own age does not in fact make biblical preaching incomprehensible or irrelevant. Indeed, I have read as much in some writings on the subject. I disagree.

Granted, there are those who have never seen a lamb, and hence to suggest that we are dumb or lost like sheep may require a bit of effort on the preacher's part. Actually, it may be more an *opportunity* than a *liability*. Often an unfamiliar image when evoked possesses a freshness of power otherwise unavailable in the well known. Otherwise put, the metaphoric tease is sometimes enhanced by imagination. As a city boy who has met more horses on television than on the farm, I remember my disappointment when finally I saw the Lone Ranger's horse on television. What a puny pony. My radio-based horse had real class. Nonetheless, whatever difficulties are presented by the differences of life between biblical days and ours are

overcome much more easily through story and narrative.
Rather than *explaining* a biblical image—as one tends to
do in topical/expository preaching—the preacher when
inside the narrative flow is more apt to provide action as a
way of *evoking* the image. So Keck, although he might have
guessed that a lot of us have never had a meal of loaves
and fish, reenacts their distribution, and all of us get fed.
His picture of the Jewish father, the blessing, and then the
disciples' waiting in line did not need any actual
familiarity on my part; he was able to count on my
imagination. Keck seems to understand that the best route
to the universal is through the depth of the particular.

Rather than logical syllogism and its definable categories of generalization and particularization, narrative
tends to focus on juxtaposition and suggestion. Hence, he
was able to bridge the gap between ancient Israel and
modern Atlanta with a single sentence: "It's that old story
again: the spies and the giants, David and Goliath, Paul in
Ephesus, Schweitzer in Lambarene, Martin Luther King in
Montgomery, you and I in Atlanta." Or again, sometimes
he names a biblical moment by means of modern language
terms, such as the disciples who "clearly believe in
responsible social action based on the contextual ethic."

The possibilities of graphic particularity and visualized
action are maximized through narrative's flow and story's
plot line. Together they assist in overcoming cultural
distance.

Narrative Techniques

Centering

As mediator between the text's story and the listeners'
experience, the crucial task for the preacher is to keep the
sermonic process on track. With one eye on the text and
the other on the listeners, the preacher is called to a joint
faithfulness. Behind the techniques of centering lie the
matters of the character and professional skill—of scholarship and pastoral sensitivity. The capacity for anticipation
is key here.

All of us have heard preachers take a sharp left turn without taking into account the fact that the congregation just took a sharp turn to the right. Perhaps the preacher wasn't aware of how it could be so or ignored the signs. And, of course, once the routes of preacher and listeners diverge, it is quite difficult to get them back on the same track. Keck anticipates well what might happen to some listeners and then utilizes means to keep the message, together with the listeners, on track. There are at least three kinds of situations that present such potential problems in this sermon. Let us review how he *avoids peripheral focus, prevents potential detours,* and *delays premature resolution.*

The very first sentence of this sermon presents a potential problem of *peripheral focus.* The imagined question, "Just what am I doing here?" could mean any number of things. Wisely Keck anticipates one possibility, that of lack of clarity of vocational call—certainly a valid issue and likely true for someone in the congregation. This happens *not* to be the issue Keck intends to address in this sermon. Hence, in the very next sentence he says so; in the third sentence he names precisely what it *is* that he will indeed address: that "gnawing demoralizing sense of inadequacy." Observe also that in this centering process he names the issue in its problematic form. He did not say, "Our purpose today is to see how Christ will enable us to conquer our sense of inadequacy." Note, however, that this straightforward "not that, but this" technique will work only *if* by naming the peripheral possible turn, it then can be released by the listeners. If the anticipated peripheral matter has greater conflict or ambiguity for the listeners, it is possible they will not be able to let go of it.

I recall that once when preaching on a text out of the Jonah story, I tried to center the issue—noting that while we are tempted to wonder what fish was around that part of the world with a stomach large enough to house a person whole, that such a digression would spoil our hearing of the text. After the worship service was over, I was greeted by a woman who said she still wondered about that. I bet she was not alone. I suspect many missed the sermon entirely. What I should have done was to center the issue by such vivid word pictures and conflict of plot that they would not have had a chance to think of the other possibility.

Again, one's capacity for word pictures can be a problem as well as an asset. If the preacher paints pictures with regular "thickness" of detail, the listeners have multiplied for them the opportunities for peripheral focus. *Paint well what you intend to be the central focus; leave the rest undetailed.*

Similar to avoiding peripheral focus is preventing *detours* of sermonic movement. We have already observed that Keck sensed that some of his listeners likely would move toward the question of identity. He not only names it but also quickly shows how such a turn is not profitable. As a result, we are centered on the road Keck is having us travel. Likewise, there are several moments when Keck is worried about our taking a detour around the issue of the miraculous. On each occasion he did three things to get us back on the right road: first, he named the possible detour; second, he brought biblical authority against it; and, third, he then used powerful detail to rivet our attention where he wanted it. Indeed, throughout the sermon Keck revealed his capacity to anticipate what might be happening to the listeners. But what if we seem to lack a good measure of that pastoral sensitivity?

I believe such sensitivity can be enhanced in us all. I suggest two specific means. First, we need to listen to audiotape recordings of our own sermons, specifically focusing on the question, Where might some listeners have taken a wrong turn? Imagine three specific listeners as the tape runs through last Sunday's sermon. Second, in case we may be unable to imagine how anyone would take a different road than the one we took, find someone, spouse or parishioner, who is willing to listen next Sunday for moments of possible detours of thought.

Finally, centering is required when the listeners want the solution too soon. In this case the preacher's task is to *delay premature resolution.* Ironically, the stronger the issue and the better presented the conflict, the more likely this will be a problem. In this sermon the problem was nearly immediate. One has to be impressed with the pastoral sensitivity reflected in Keck's choice of theme. Given the context of a seminary chapel experience, what more relevant issue could be chosen? Moreover, his crisp description of all the ramifications of the problem cries out for resolution. Keck knows that the Synoptic text is going to deliver that resolution. *Yet the text is first introduced as a problem, not as a solution.* We find out just how parallel the disciples' problem is to ours; indeed, we must live through their experience before the solution is presented. In order to delay resolution, Keck centers our attention to those aspects of the text that exacerbate the problem.

Language Use

Beyond our noticing the effective use of language demonstrated in this sermon by Keck, there are two special kinds of language use we should note briefly. Both have a kind of shock or surprise. The first is the use of the metaphoric tease in an unsuspecting place. Not only does Keck speak of our gnawing sense of inadequacy with the strong term "terror," he also describes it as it happening in the "night", a word that has the double referent of time of day and state of soul. The double meaning provides a shock to the system. More impressive still is the way he catches us off-guard by putting strange words in unlikely places. One could call the use of the phrase "contextual ethic" in reference to the disciples an anachronism. I call it power. It becomes a metaphor through time rather than a metaphor through space. He does not do this because contextual ethics are in any way central to this sermon. He does it to make a statement about the universality of human experience. Certainly he could have made some claim of connection by means of discursive thought. Rather, quite quickly he puts strange words in an unlikely place. What economy of language! Likewise, in reenacting Paul's experience of inadequacy, he provides a short conversation between Jesus and Paul. Of course, we know this is an inventive moment in the sermon. What we are not prepared for is the powerful shock which occurs when Keck "violates" the time frame and says: "The same Lord who did not get nervous when he looked down at the little lunch said to Paul, 'My power is made perfect in your five loaves.' " In *Paul's* five loaves? Exactly.

Rhythm

The sense of timing in this sermon is remarkable. Since we have had occasion to reflect on it by means of the running commentary, we will only note it in passing now. But it needs to be named here as one of Keck's more important techniques. Pacing is critical.

Of course, a sermon must move at varying rates of speed, geared to highlight and enflesh the important moments as well as to avoid the boredom that accompanies too steady a pace. A sermon also must give listeners time to absorb the content, to pause for transition, even to rest momentarily in order to gain energy for the next engagement of thought. These appear second nature for our preacher.

Recall the first portion of the sermon, how after absorbing our interest and capturing our energy regarding our sense of inadequacy, he pauses. Surely he must know that if he presses further, our circuits of self may get blown. It is painful to have your soul exposed so articulately. With the phrase "In other words" he begins to summarize the problem. The opening phrase reassures us that he is not going press the details of our malady further; he is just going to state it succinctly for us. This gives us a chance to catch our breath. And the summary provides us the chance to see the matter with more objective distance. Counselors do the same in their therapeutic settings.

Later in the sermon Keck comes to that moment when the good news of the gospel is evoked, and we learn how, out of such meager resources, by the transforming power of Jesus' blessing all are fed. Now, how are the listeners to know the cruciality of this moment in the sermon? One might answer that it is obviously so and stated ever so crisply. How could one miss it? But we forget that attention comes in waves—I think not in either-or components but in more-and-less connections. If this happened to be a moment of less connection for a listener, it might be missed altogether. We who have now experienced only the written "remains" of the lived experience may forget that written material is always available for a look back. With oral address, it vanishes into the silence. Hence, Keck repeats the good news for a full thirty seconds by my timing.

In my experience in listening professionally to sermons for over twenty-five years, I would rank lack of repetition at such crucial moments as the third most frequent problem (the first being not including the good news and the second being not connecting the good news to our situation). *Such watershed moments in the sermon simply must be pointed.* Keck's use of repetition is clear in the manuscript. I suspect, had I actually heard the sermon, that this effective repetition was also underscored by a difference in such vocal factors as pitch, quality, rate, and volume.

Narrative Norms

Biblical Methodology

We should not be surprised that this outstanding professor of New Testament has much to teach us through the occasion of this sermon about faithful and effective utilization of the Scripture in narrative preaching. The first has to do with faithfulness to the text. In part we considered it previously, in the discussion about place-ment of the preacher. I believe it can be described as the preacher's self-conscious understanding of occupying the *servant role.* Clearly, Keck always stood under the text. This is always implicit; sometimes it is made explicit. For example, when he says, "That story illumines where we find ourselves," it is evident that our preacher identifies himself with us, not the text. He claims to being addressed by it as much as we are. Of course, he has only just now read the text, not yet interpreted it. And there are many who might say such a thing and then by an attitude that slips in between the lines reveal a doctrinaire and authoritarian stance. Not here.

What makes his claim credible is that it is *not* followed by the dispensing of a grocery list of exegetical intricacies served up prior to our engagement with the text. Indeed, after acknowledging that it is not easy to "get with the beat of this story," he very quickly says, "But, back to the story." Immediately he and we are immersed in the disciples' situation, which draws attention away from the preacher as expert mediator. In short, being drawn into the Synoptic story keeps us from noticing who it is whose words are the vehicle of our immersion. The more any preacher keeps the listeners *inside* the story instead of directing the listeners to look *at* the story, the less dominant the preacher remains. Note how, after Keck has taken us through the story—even including the initial proclamation of the good news—he says, "Mark's picture is coming through now." Still he is listener—in a sense the first of all the listeners. It is a servant role.

At the same time, however, he does not camouflage his role as interpreter by allowing us to think his telling of the story is without editorial contribution. He owns up to the detail he utilizes. He will say, for example, "To paraphrase . . . " and, again, "I can put it this way." Such *ownership of the interpretative role* is key to effective biblical preaching. It can enflesh a story without involving the kind of eisegesis that happens when listeners are not cued as to what came directly out of the text and what is interpretively included. Moreover, it is not only important to cue folks about our creative additions or interpretations, it is also important to *stop* doing it. Can you imagine how wooden the rendering of the story would have been had Keck always inserted "To paraphrase . . . " or "I can put it this way"? Once the congregation is made aware of the interpretive style being utilized, the preacher then needs simply to *do it, not talk about doing it.* That is why Keck did not alert us to the fictional component of Jesus talking to Paul about his loaves. Keck was free not only to be creative in the telling of the story but also even to raise difficult questions of the text—even of Jesus.

If you have ever had a member of a congregation say to you regarding a just-completed sermon, "You know, I've always wondered about that text," chances are you raised a difficult question lay people have wanted to ask but haven't had the nerve to. They become grateful for you to do it. Such sermonic moments are of greater importance than the point of the particular sermon. Such moments grant permission to people to engage the biblical witness, not just to swallow it dutifully. Keck served as an important role model here when he raised questions, even about Jesus' relation with reality.

These, then, are three features of biblical narrative methodology that Keck's sermon brings to light: the servant role of the interpreter, candid ownership of enfleshed interpretations, and the probing spirit of biblical work that brings the text alive in the listeners' experience.

Placement of Redemptive Power

One of the "bottom-line" questions that must be asked of any sermon is: Who or what made the difference today? When listeners come away from a sermon noting how clever or effective the preacher was, you can bet that the sermonic aim was not completely realized. There must be a transparency in our work. Keck would have been disappointed had a student left chapel that day with some such remark as "You really know how to explain things." My hunch is that such a remark did not happen, although surely not a few students were grateful that the preacher did. The point is that our inadequacies, if solved by the evocation of the sermon, are solved by the power of Christ's blessing. Nothing less can be any sermon's purpose.

This is not only true in general regarding the overall

impact of the sermon, it likewise is true at specific moments. In the context of the biblical stories—from both Mark and Paul—the placement of the preacher on the receiving end of the text/listener relationship is crucial. But note also how this is true of the concluding illustrations. Even when they cannot name it precisely, people are sensitive to preachers who come out as heroes in their own stories. Such denials as "No credit to me, you understand; I simply was an instrument of the Lord" simply will not do. Note in his illustration that it was not Keck's *faithfulness* that was utilized by God but his *inadequacy*. In the second illustration, it is an unnamed student who is involved. All of this is, of course, Keck's point—that it "is not what happened to the bread but what happened to the people when the bread was blessed." The basic rule or norm here is simply that the redemptive power of any sermon does not come *from* the preacher—it comes *to* the preacher. Throughout this sermon our preacher seemed the first recipient of the good news. The purpose of the sermon was simply to widen the circle of Jesus' blessing.

We have now "heard" and seen one biblical story determine the shape of the narrative sermon in the narrative design called *running the story*. And we have experienced another narrative sermon model that begins with the world of the congregation and then turns to the biblical story—an illustration of *delaying the story*.

We will now consider a third option in biblical narrative preaching, namely, *suspending the story*.

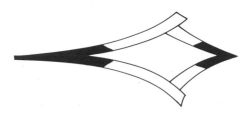

Suspending the Story

This sermon will begin inside the text, run into a problem, and hence require the telling of that story to be suspended while another text provides a way out of the dilemma. Once accomplished, the sermonic process moves back to the central text for the completion of the message.

Listen, then, for my sermonic offering in *suspending the story*.

(Please read out loud.)

"Who Could Ask for Anything More?"
by
Eugene L. Lowry

For the kingdom of heaven is like a householder who went out early in the morning to hire laborers for his vineyard. After agreeing with the laborers for a denarius a day, he sent them into his vineyard. And going out about the third hour he saw others standing idle in the market place; and to them he said, "You go into the vineyard too, and whatever is right I will give you." So they went. Going out again about the sixth hour and the ninth hour, he did the same. And about the eleventh hour he went

out and found others standing; and he said to them,
"Why do you stand here idle all day?" They said to him,
"Because no one has hired us." He said to them, "You go
into the vineyard too." And when evening came, the
owner of the vineyard said to his steward, "Call the
laborers and pay them their wages, beginning with the
last, up to the first." And when those hired about the
eleventh hour came, each of them received a denarius.
Now when the first came, they thought they would
receive more; but each of them also received a denarius.
And on receiving it they grumbled at the householder,
saying, "These last worked only one hour, and you have
made them equal to us who have borne the burden of the
day and the scorching heat." But he replied to one of
them, "Friend, I am doing you no wrong; did you not
agree with me for a denarius? Take what belongs to you,
and go; I choose to give to this last as I give to you. Am I
not allowed to do what I choose with what belongs to
me? Or do you begrudge my generosity?" So the last will
be first, and the first last. (Matthew 20:1-16)

It was about a quarter of seven in the morning when
the owner of the vineyard went to the marketplace to hire
workers for the day. They all agreed on a denarius for the
day's labor—a reasonable amount. So they went to
work. About a quarter till nine, the owner was back at the
marketplace—the equivalent of a town square. Finding
others there looking for work, the owner said, "whatever
is right I will pay you," and they went to work. About a
quarter till twelve, the owner is back at the marketplace—and one wonders why he didn't hire all he
needed the first time. Perhaps a storm was coming. And
they too go to work. Again, about a quarter till three he's
back again—and once more at quarter till five—when
there's only one hour of work left.

Now it's six o'clock—and time to be paid. The owner
whispers (I think) in the ear of the financial steward of the
corporation to pay the last ones first. And they have to be
surprised. They have worked only one hour—yet they

receive a full denarius. They are ecstatic—but not half as much as those who came at seven. "You mean he's going to pay one denarius for each hour's work? Why, that's almost a half month's salary for us." They can't believe it, but they do—until the steward begins paying those who came at three. There's some mistake here. They're getting the same amount. Surely the owner will whisper in the steward's ear again, correcting the mistake.

But he doesn't, and by this time the steward is paying the twelve o'clock folks—and still giving each just one denarius. Smiles have faded from seven o'clock faces. "You mean he going to pay everybody the same amount, regardless of how much work?" Unbelievable—really unthinkable.

Sure enough, those who came at seven receive just one denarius. The text says they "grumbled"—surely a modest way to put it. (Probably couldn't print what they really said.) "What do you mean, paying us the same as all the rest? Why, those last folks hardly had time to work up a sweat, yet you make them equal to those of us who have borne the burden of the day and the scorching noontime heat."

"Now, wait just a minute, here" the owner responds. "Why should you expect any more? Don't I remember a conversation we had about a quarter till seven this morning? Didn't you agree to work for a denarius?" "Well, yes, of course, but it's all different now, when we see you pay those others the same. Of course we expect more." "What's the matter—you begrudge my generosity? I choose to pay them the same. I take it that's my business, isn't it? It's my money. You—take your denarius, and get out of here."

Well, I must say—I think they've got a point, don't you? I mean, imagine you came to work at seven—how do you feel just now? What's *right* here has to do with relative justice, among *all* the workers. And the truth is, if you are a public employer, indeed you do *not* have a right to "do as you please" with your money.

So you're on the school board in your town, about to hire a couple new teachers. Both have the same fine college records, same experience. One male, the other female. You plan to pay the woman less because of the conditions of the job market? You'd better not. Somebody's going to be breathing down your neck, and they ought to be. Going to hire a couple folks to do some yard work—one white, the other black? Same experience. Going to pay the black person less because you can get away with it? Well, it's wrong.

This story is the same kind of issue, just in different form. I say, this is a good case for the National Labor Relations Board, don't you think? In fact, I'm shocked. Why on earth would Jesus take the side of an unjust owner? In fact, you know, that business of paying the last ones first . . . that was cruel—and it was dumb. He forced the seven o'clock folks to watch while the injustice was being perpetrated. He'd been a whole lot better off to pay the seven o'clock folks first—get them out of his hair—then nine, then twelve. Nobody would ever know. Besides, what's going to happen to the owner tomorrow morning? He's going to go down to the marketplace about a quarter till seven—and guess what? Nobody's there. He'd better come back about a quarter till five—lots of folks there then, ready for work.

There must be something peculiar going on in this story; otherwise, I just don't understand. Well, yes, there is, and our first clue was the scene of the last ones paid first. But you really can't get the gist of the story unless you go back one chapter in Matthew.

Remember the scene? Jesus is having a conversation with the one we have come to call the rich young ruler, who seems to have his life in order except for one thing. Jesus says, "Go, sell everything, and give it all to the poor—and then come back."

Well, the disciples are listening to this encounter, and they can't believe their ears. They have just returned from a church growth seminar and cannot believe that Jesus would let such an outstanding prospect get away.

Jesus sees their shock and says, "I tell you, it is easier for a camel to get through the eye of a needle than for a rich man to get into the kingdom." And don't try to demythologize the image here—with the eye representing the gate to the city. No, Jesus means exactly what he says: It is easier for a big fat camel—humps and all—to get through the eye of a little needle than for a rich person to get into the kingdom.

"Well, that's impossible," they say, and they are certainly on target *here*. Jesus gives them the good news: "Well, with people it is impossible, but with God, all things are possible." But they miss it altogether, and Simon Peter comes waltzing up, one foot in his mouth, and says, "But Jesus, we have left everything to follow you—what do we get?" Hear it? "We've left everything to follow you—what do we get?"

And the answer? *Cheated.* That's what you get. The kingdom is not a business deal, not a contract, but a covenant. If you start asking, "What's the bottom line for me?" the answer is simple: cheated.

And immediately following this account is the story of the workers in the vineyard, so we *all* will know just how cheated we're going to be. And of course, I never compare myself with those who have done more than I. I compare myself with those who have done less.

And this "bottom-line" mentality has troubled the church ever since. I remember as a child in a small Methodist church in Wichita, Kansas, listening in on the old folks' conversation. One such conversation went like this: "You know . . . it's just not fair. You mean to tell me that we who have been faithful to the church, given our money and time, always lived the straight and narrow—you mean to tell me that when we get to heaven, we'll be joined there by that guy who's always done whatever he wanted, really lived it up, until his deathbed conversion experience? You mean the same heaven? Just isn't fair."

Sometimes the attitude comes in tragic form. You're at an area-wide church leadership training event on a Sunday afternoon. They divide you up into small groups and direct you to the proper room and a circle of chairs. Most of the folks you don't know. So the leader says, "Suppose we start by going around the circle and introduce ourselves. Just tell us who you are." You go around the circle until you come to this older man who says, "My name is . . . and I used to be a plumber." "Used to be?" What does he mean *used to be?* You hear it? Life is a contract, and his contract ran out. He used to be a person, brought home the bacon. But now, he is a "used to be."

You keep going around the circle until you come to this woman, who looks up sheepishly and says, "Well, I'm just a housewife." *Just?* What does that mean? It means that she doesn't bring home the bacon either. Now, she has to cook it and clean up after it, and all the rest of an eighteen-hour day, but the contract is a bit fuzzy, you know. "I'm just a housewife."

Now, I want to ask you to imagine that today you are the parent of three children—three, six, and nine years of age. Now, do you love the nine-year-old three times as much as the three-year-old, because, of course, the eldest has been three times as much help around the house? You, who are nine years old—do you love your parents three times as much as you did when you were three? "Why," you say, "that's ridiculous. We're family." Exactly. This is family. So's the story. Jesus was talking about a family covenant. Simon thought it was a business deal.

And do you know where that vineyard owner is this very minute? Why, he's back at the marketplace, looking to see if there is anyone else who has not yet heard the invitation, not yet had the chance to respond.

So you see, it doesn't really matter whether the invitation comes at seven, or nine, or noon, or three, or five, or two till.

To be invited into the vineyard is to be invited home. Who could ask for anything more?

Having experienced this illustration of the biblical

narrative design *suspending the story,* let us move quickly to our homiletical exegesis.

Running Commentary

It was about a quarter of seven in the morning when the owner of the vineyard went to the marketplace to hire workers for the day. They all agreed on a denarius for the day's labor—a reasonable amount. So they went to work. About a quarter till nine, the owner was back at the marketplace, the equivalent to a town square. Finding others there looking for work, the owner said, "whatever is right I will pay you," and they went to work. About a quarter till twelve, the owner is back at the marketplace, and one wonders why he didn't hire all he needed the first time. Perhaps a storm was coming. And they too go to work. Again, about a quarter till three he's back again, and once more at quarter till five, when there's only one hour of work left.

The sermon begins inside the story line of the text. The paraphrase is "tight," that is, does not stray far from the rendering of the text itself. Changes consist primarily of updating the way things are said. Then why paraphrase at all? Why not read the text in a modern translation? The reasons are threefold. First, I want to reinforce the text by an additional rendering. Second, a paraphrase has the effect of saying to the listeners, "This story is close at hand, not remote and hence difficult to comprehend." Third, soon the preacher will begin to add detail, even enflesh it through imagined data. To begin with a tight paraphrase sets the stage for that further development. One small editorial addition is given in order for the listeners to picture the marketplace scene. Once I put one foot outside the story, with "one wonders . . ." My purpose is to foreshadow a later stage in the sermon when I question the judgment of the owner. I want the listeners used to the idea of such questioning.

Now it's six o'clock, and time to be paid. The owner whispers (I think) in the ear of the financial steward of the

*corporation to pay the last ones first. And they have to be
surprised. They have worked only one hour, yet they
receive a full denarius. They are ecstatic, but not half as
much as those who came at seven. "You mean he's going
to pay one denarius for each hour's work? Why, that's
almost a half month's salary for us." They can't believe it,
but they do—until the steward begins paying those who
came at three. There's some mistake here. They're getting
the same amount. Surely the owner will whisper in the
steward's ear again, correcting the mistake.*

The preacher doesn't have to work at complicating the
story line. Jesus already has. Very quickly it is pay time,
and I begin to add imaginative detail (the owner
"whispers"). Because those listeners who have heard the
reading of the text know what is about to happen and are
already "looking" at those who came at seven o'clock, I try
both to detour and delay. Hence, I call attention to the
latecomers and their surprise. Then I shift the focus back
to the seven o'clock workers, but to a time earlier than the
moment of their being paid. The purpose here is twofold.
First, I want the listeners inside the experience of those
who worked all day, in order to make credible their
complaint. Second, I hope to increase the tension.

*But he doesn't, and by this time the steward is paying the
twelve o'clock folks and still giving each just one denarius.
Smiles have faded from seven o'clock faces. "You mean he
going to pay everybody the same amount, regardless of
how much work?" Unbelievable—really unthinkable.*

Purposely I am slowing the pace, which always has its
dangers. Slowing the pace for heightened tension is most
likely to work either when there is action that can be
imagined or crisp description that can be utilized. Again, I
am attempting to build their case by using the term
"unthinkable," which I hope will find resonance with the
listeners.

Sure enough, those who came at seven receive just one denarius. The text says they "grumbled"—surely a modest way to put it. (Probably couldn't print what they really said.) "What do you mean, paying us the same as all the rest? Why, those last folks hardly had time to work up a sweat, yet you make them equal to those of us who have borne the burden of the day and the scorching noontime heat."

But the moment of injustice happens as we knew it would. The text provides a marvelous understatement: "They grumbled." Since I have been paraphrasing the story just now, I have to momentarily step outside to refer to the text. Note that my editorial comment on the understatement is itself an understatement: "surely a *modest* way to put it."

Whenever a preacher decides to step outside the story line for a reference to the text, the listeners need a strong line to get back in. Dialogue is a good technique. Hence, I said, "What do you mean . . . ?"

"Now, wait just a minute, here" the owner responds. "Why should you expect any more? Don't I remember a conversation we had about a quarter till seven this morning? Didn't you agree to work for a denarius?" "Well, yes, of course, but it's all different now, when we see you pay those others the same. Of course we expect more." "What's the matter—you begrudge my generosity? I choose to pay them the same. I take it that's my business, isn't it? It's my money. You . . . take your denarius, and get out of here."

The owner's question about why should they expect more is a method both of encapsulating their position and making an ever-so-brief reference to the title of the sermon.

The extensive use of dialogue, such as occurs here, raises a critical issue. One must not stay in dialogue long or listeners will begin to perceive a "little drama" going on and will back off to see how well the preacher can act. Bad news. Here, I was pushing my luck a bit.

Well, I must say, I think they've got a point, don't you? I mean, imagine you came to work at seven—how do you feel just now? What's right here has to do with relative justice, among all the workers. And the truth is, if you are a public employer, indeed you do not have a right to "do as you please" with your money.

The biblical story is now finished. We are not through with it, of course, because it leaves us with a problem of understanding rather than a tidy conclusion. At this point I take a step to one side and invite the listeners to join me in scrutinizing the moment in question. Indeed, I call for a decision *for* the workers and *against* the owner. For the first time I refer to the listeners and address them as "you."

So you're on the school board in your town, about to hire a couple new teachers. Both have the same fine college records, same experience. One male, the other female. You plan to pay the woman less because of the conditions of the job market? You'd better not. Somebody's going to be breathing down your neck, and they ought to be. Going to hire a couple folks to do some yard work—one white, the other black? Same experience. Going to pay the black person less because you can get away with it? Well, it's wrong.

You can tell that I am not certain the listeners are going to concur with my judgment. I think my assumption here is well founded. People know the owner is the hero in the story and that Jesus is the one telling it. Given these factors, there is a reluctance to go against the grain here. But if we don't, the story will not be pushed to the point where the good news of the gospel can be proclaimed later. Hence, I move away from the biblical context for a couple of imagined contemporary moments. I have tried to set the scenes in such a way that the conclusion is inevitable, at least for most listeners.

This story is the same kind of issue, just in different form. I say, this is a good case for the National Labor Relations Board, don't you think? In fact, I'm shocked.

Why on earth would Jesus take the side of an unjust owner? In fact, you know, that business of paying the last ones first . . . that was cruel—and it was dumb. He forced the seven o'clock folks to watch while the injustice was being perpetrated. He'd been a whole lot better off to pay the seven o'clock folks first—get them out of his hair—then nine, then twelve. Nobody would ever know. Besides, what's going to happen to the owner tomorrow morning? He's going to go down to the marketplace about a quarter till seven—and guess what? Nobody's there. He'd better come back about a quarter till five—lots of folks there then, ready for work.

Of course, there will be a few who are not so sure of my conclusion. What can a preacher do? One approach is to attempt a phrase that will capture others' possible conclusion while at the same time restating the preacher's. "Why on earth would Jesus take the side of an unjust owner?" is just such a phrase. It could mean "It *couldn't* be unjust. Why on earth would Jesus . . . ?" It could mean "Yes, indeed, it *is* unjust. Why on earth . . . ?" With either interpretation the term "why" serves to move things along. Everyone is encouraged to probe the matter a bit more to see what further light might be shed. Sometimes at such crucial turning points in a plot line, a touch of humor brings folks together, which I attempt in observing what will happen to the owner tomorrow. Moreover, in addition, I note the fact that the owner had another more logical option in paying the workers. All in all, I am attempting to reinforce the absurdity of the scene and hence to lure the listeners toward further exploration.

There must be something peculiar going on in this story; otherwise, I just don't understand. Well, yes, there is, and our first clue was the scene of the last ones paid first. But you really can't get the gist of the story unless you go back one chapter in Matthew.

Here is the moment of suspension, toward which we have been building for some time. The biblical story simply is not internally self-evident, at least in terms we know now. I point to a clue given by Jesus' telling and flash back to the previous chapter in Matthew.

> *Remember the scene? Jesus is having a conversation with the one we have come to call the rich young ruler, who seems to have his life in order except for one thing. Jesus says, "Go, sell everything, and give it all to the poor—and then come back."*

Whether the listeners go with the preacher at a moment of suspension depends upon whether a sufficiently ambiguous problem is evoked. In addition, it is helpful if there is some intrinsic interest in that to which all are invited to attend. We are lucky that the text in which resolution is sought happens to be a story.

> *Well, the disciples are listening to this encounter, and they can't believe their ears. They have just returned from a church growth seminar and cannot believe that Jesus would let such an outstanding prospect get away. Jesus sees their shock and says, "I tell you, it is easier for a camel to get through the eye of a needle than for a rich man to get into the kingdom." And don't try to demythologize the image here, with the eye representing the gate to the city. No, Jesus means exactly what he says: it is easier for a big fat camel—humps and all—to get through the eye of a little needle than for a rich person to get into the kingdom.*

So we are now in the middle of this prior story, which becomes a subplot or pre-plot. By now, the listeners must have sufficient reason to stay tuned—reason based on the interest generated by this episode. Their major focus of attention is here, not directly upon why and how they got here. To be sure, there should be a vague sense of the workers' story, but if too much the listeners will not attend to the rich young ruler. Sometimes a biblical story cannot be suspended because its force is so great listeners "refuse" to enter a subplot.

Were it the case that the narrative suspension moved to another text that was *not* in story form, the listeners would need an occasional reminder of the reason for the apparent digression.

"Well, that's impossible," they say, and they are certainly on target here. Jesus gives them the good news: "Well, with people it is impossible, but with God, all things are possible." But they miss it altogether, and Simon Peter comes waltzing up, one foot in his mouth, and says, "But Jesus, we have left everything to follow you—what do we get?" Hear it? "We've left everything to follow you—what do we get?"

Typically, I have referred to the "distance" between the preacher and the biblical story in such terms as *inside the story, one foot outside* (meaning with an occasional editorial comment, such as my reference to "demythologizing"), or *looking at the story.* This section is a bit different and not easily described. Note that we are both *in* the story and yet also editorializing *within* it—for example, "Jesus gives them the good news . . . but they miss it."

And the answer? Cheated. That's what you get. The kingdom is not a business deal, not a contract, but a covenant. If you start asking, "What's the bottom line for me?" the answer is simple: cheated.

"Cheated"—this word is the axis around which the entire sermonic reversal turns. To be sure, it will need definition by some further discussion about *contract* and *covenant,* but these latter terms are not memorable or strong. *Cheated* is.

And immediately following this account is the story of the workers in the vineyard, so we all will know just how cheated we're going to be. And of course, I never compare myself with those who have done more than I. I compare myself with those who have done less.

Note, here, that I did *not* say that "Jesus immediately tells," because that would be poor exegetical work. Probably a redactor placed the story here. But I did allow listeners to infer it, did I not? I confess—but justify it on the grounds that the redactor simply perceived the connection between Peter's question and Jesus' parable.

And this "bottom-line" mentality has troubled the church ever since. I remember as a child in a small Methodist church in Wichita, Kansas, listening in on the old folks' conversation. One such conversation went like this: "You know . . . it's just not fair. You mean to tell me that we who have been faithful to the church, given our money and time, always lived the straight and narrow—you mean to tell me that when we get to heaven, we'll be joined there by that guy who's always done whatever he wanted, really lived it up, until his deathbed conversion experience? You mean the same heaven? Just isn't fair."

So we arrive at "mentality"—a term always used for a point of view with which we disagree. With it I launch into a contemporary story to help folks identify with this contractual thinking. In telling this story I violate a principle of mine, which is not to make a point and *then* illustrate it but rather to utilize a story *to make* the point. In this case, however, it was a biblical story that made the point—and we missed it—until Peter "helped" us. And because the story is so recognizable by many church folks, I believe it brings Peter to our time. All of which is to say, that in any given sermon, the preacher is caught with multiple norms or principles. None are absolute, and all must be weighed in relative terms. If not, we become paralyzed in our work.

Sometimes the attitude comes in tragic form. You're at an area-wide church leadership training program on a Sunday afternoon. They divide you up into small groups and direct you to the proper room and a circle of chairs. Most of the folks you don't know. So the leader says, "Suppose we start by going around the circle and introduce ourselves. Just tell us who you are." You go around the circle until you come to this older man who says, "My name is . . . and I used to be a plumber." "Used to be?" What does he mean used to be? You hear it? Life is a contract, and his contract ran out.

He used to be a person, brought home the bacon. But now, he is a "used to be."

Note that the attitude appeal changes here. The matter is named not simply as *wrong* but as *tragic*. I am appealing here for the pathos it deserves. In my description of the Sunday afternoon meeting, I am presuming that its utility here is not dependent upon whether everyone has been to such a meeting. Imagination is not as limited as experience. And in my description of that experience I am attempting to associate the word "contract" with "bringing home the bacon" and "used to be."

This imagined situation also provides me the opportunity to address "in passing" another related issue, that is, the source of so much of the trouble many people have with retirement.

You keep going around the circle until you come to this woman, who looks up sheepishly and says, "Well, I'm just a housewife." Just? What does that mean? It means that she doesn't bring home the bacon either. Now, she has to cook it and clean up after it, and all the rest of an eighteen-hour day, but the contract is a bit fuzzy, you know. "I'm just a housewife."

Likewise, the issue of gender fits exactly our discussion of the limitation of the contract "mentality." Here I continue my association of terms and phrases by linking "bacon," "contract," and "just a housewife."

In short, this biblical text and sermon have larger ramifications than the issue of heaven and who ought to go there. They deal with an underlying mentality that affects our entire life-style. Had I directed a sermonic critique on the American dream, likely it would not have been heard. Obviously, I am hoping this more indirect method might gain a hearing.

Now, I want to ask you to imagine that today you are the parent of three children—three, six, and nine years of age. Now, do you love the nine-year-old three times as much as the three-year-old, because, of course, the eldest has been three times as much help around the house? You, who are nine years old—do you love your parents three times as much as you did when you were three? "Why," you say, "that's ridiculous. We're family." Exactly. This is family. So's the story. Jesus was talking about a family covenant. Simon thought it was a business deal.

Just as "cheated" was supposed to evoke the negative side of the contract/covenant equation, so "family" now is intended to evoke the positive side. Otherwise put, the sermonic "aha" or reversal is now restated.

Unlike most sermons, which move us toward new or newly named behavior that grows out of the proclamation of the gospel, this sermon does not. By this illustration I am presuming that the problem is not in knowing how to behave but on what grounds.

And do you know where that vineyard owner is this very minute? Why, he's back at the marketplace, looking to see if there is anyone else who has not yet heard the invitation, not yet had the chance to respond.

The sermon could end here without this final imagined scene. I have stated what I wanted to say, and I trust the meaning is fairly clear. But for some time now we have been *talking about* things, through discourse and illustration. The truth of the gospel is more easily *evoked* when the preacher is *in the story line*. So I reenter the story so the owner can make another pass by the marketplace. To do so is to claim that the world still is operating on the basis of Jesus' story.

So you see, it doesn't really matter whether the invitation comes at seven, or nine, or noon, or three, or five, or two till.

To be invited into the vineyard is to be invited home.

Obviously, the key words here are "invited home."

Who could ask for anything more?

I close with the title and hope that when folks see the television commercial that closes with this line, they will receive the sermon all over again.

Narrative Capabilities, Techniques, and Norms

Once again we will review some of the various narrative features that are operating in the sermon—in this case, "Who Could Ask for Anything More?"

Narrative Capabilities

Variation of Content Shape

The sweep of narrativity, from opening conflict through increased complication to the fundamental turn (called peripetia) and finally into denouement, makes possible variations of content shape and movement that are unthinkable in other forms of discourse. Its logic is born of the torque of suspense, drawn from the ideas, to be sure, but not from the internal logic of the ideas themselves. Even the shape of dialectical thought, with its thesis, antithesis, and synthesis, while more "narrative" in its logic, is nonetheless fairly constrained.

The principle of ambiguity, which gives shape to narrative process, *as principle* lies outside the dynamics of any particular line of reasoning. Its application makes possible a wide range of moves. More simply stated, if there is a piece of data that needs to be included in a sermon, you simply "allow," even "nudge," the thought into the corner that requires that data. More often it happens the other way around—namely, the material with which you are dealing runs into a problem that it seems unable to handle. The preacher must find help to surmount the difficulty in order to go on, which is exactly what happened in the preparation for this sermon. Indeed, I first chose the text because I couldn't understand it. Once I began wrestling with its problem, I followed my own advice to engage in further biblical work before and after the text itself. It was then that I found Peter asking his self-serving question. I knew then the focus, turn, and aim of the sermon, although I didn't know quite how it would all happen. So I ran the workers' story until it hit its problem, suspended the story, and temporarily jumped back into the previous story. For comparison we might take a look at the more "logical" way (in the narrow sense) one might have done it.

In light of the fact that the Simon episode comes first *and* is needed in order to understand the workers' tale, one could start with Simon. It seems the reasonable thing to do. Simon is selfish, thinks the kingdom is a contract, and needs to be set straight. The workers' story will do it nicely. But do you notice that this method lacks heightened suspense? The answer is given early, and the rest is explanation. When placed in this order, even the story form of the workers' episode lacks suspense. "Oh, yes, of course, here (in advance) is the reason we're about to hear it."

There are other possibilities, of course. The point here is that the option of suspending a story relies on the opportunity *anticipation* provides. People will give the preacher a decent chance to explain something *if* they have been cued as to its "necessity."

The inductive method of adding specifics 1, 2, 3, and 4 to result in the generalized A has some suspense but little surprise. The deductive method of explaining that because of generalized A the consequent specifics of 1, 2, 3, and 4 naturally follow lacks both suspense and surprise.

This might be an appropriate time to note that this suspension of a story does not limit the preacher to a flash*back* to a previous text. I could have "flashed out" to a topical discussion of contract and covenant without utilizing the Peter episode at all. Or I could have "flashed into" a family story that would tellingly evoke this sense of covenant. To suspend the story simply means to temporarily halt the telling of the central biblical story long enough to get help. Lucky for me, there Peter stood, and did it all.

Alternation Between Engagement with Text and with Listeners

By means of Keck's sermon we noted how the preacher is related both to the text and to the listeners. Our focus there had to do with *where* the preacher's identity was in all this. Noting again the dual relation of preacher to text and to listeners, our concern here is with the mode of presentation. Narrative process facilitates nicely an alternating direction of *presence* on the part of the preacher. Sometimes, for example, the preacher is *engaging the people*; other times the preacher is *engaging the text*.

When I began the sermon, I simply began telling the tale. I wasn't *talking to* the people. It was as though they were eavesdropping on my conversation with the biblical material. This direction of presence is more easily experienced than named. For example, had you been physically present for the actual sermon, you would have noted that my eye contact is different during such times of engaging the text. Perhaps the power of storytelling lies in part in the perceived sense of indirection. It feels almost illicit. No wonder listeners seem to pay more attention. Then when the preacher turns directly to the congregation (as I did with the words "Well, I must say—I think they've got a point, don't you?") there is a communicational shock. The eyes reveal it, and the listeners sense it. The relational mode is altered fundamentally. And these are not the only two modes.

For example, there is a difference between running inside the story and commenting upon it. It is as though the preacher is facing a slightly different direction in each mode of communication. We will return to this later as we discuss "lateral movement." Right now, the important thing to note is the variety of modes, and hence variety of presentation, facilitated by means of narrative form.

Inclusion of "Controversial" Ingredients

My past experience as a topical preacher while in the parish led me to be quite forthright about preaching on controversial issues. During the sixties I remember well that sense of call to be responsible in my pastoral preaching. I tried to be faithful. *And* I always approached such sermons in the same manner: I preached *on* controversial issues. Then a remarkable thing happened to me.

I had just announced by special mailing the beginning of a series of sermons on the parables. I remember they were entitled "People Pictures." Unexpectedly, one nationally current controversial issue arose within the life of the congregation itself. I was tempted to drop my planned series and address the issue, as it was going to engage the church board soon. I planned no equivocation on the issue. We were going to face it head on. Then either good pastoral judgment or cowardice intervened, and I decided to go ahead with my previously planned series on the parables.

Although a visitor during those four weeks likely would not have known a storm was brewing in the life of the congregation, and although the visitors would never have heard that issue preached *on*, nonetheless, that issue permeated the preaching of those four weeks. Either by implication or passing reference, we did indeed confront that issue.

Narrative preaching, when it involves a biblical story, provides a way of *engaging an issue while talking about another subject.*" The "other subject," of course, is the biblical story. The result is less defensiveness on the part of the listeners and a less authoritarian stand on the part of the preacher. Moreover, the "heat" of controversy is absorbed by the story instead of being absorbed by the preacher.

Although such potentially controversial issues as were reflected in this present sermon were only briefly mentioned and were not related centrally, the principle is nonetheless evident here. Picking up on our immediately previous discussion, issues that are hard to hear often can be heard best when the preacher is "facing" the *text* rather than "facing" the *congregation.*

Narrative Techniques

Paraphrasing

We have already observed three reasons for paraphrasing a narrative text: to reinforce the text by an additional rendering, to communicate indirectly that the story is not as remote as it might at first appear, and to commence listener expectations toward later elaboration. Here we focus on the advantages of beginning with a "tight" paraphrase before moving toward more elaborate embellishments. The issues are those of trust and commitment.

Often I find myself unwilling to read a feature story in the newspaper. The headline is interesting, but the lead line reads, "It was a crisp evening in March." Do you sense my wavering spirit here? In a single opening phrase the writer has told me that (1) the writer is going to do a clever piece here, (2) it will include elaborate embellishment, and (3) it is going to take quite a while to get to the meat of the article. Well, I am not sure I want to take the trip. Before the writer can gain my commitment, I must grant considerable trust in the hope that it will be worth my time and effort.

Suppose I had begun the last paragraph with "These issues can be raised by going with me to the evening newspaper." Now, I would be saying the same thing, but it certainly has a different feel.

When the preacher begins the sermon with a much-embellished first sentence (often a description of the setting,) the listener immediately calculates the likely time to be committed, just as I used to time the first point in an expected three-point sermon. Better to begin simply, without suggesting what a rugged journey this is going to be. That is why the beginning of my sermon included tight paraphrasing only. Then, after people have made the preliminary commitment to "go for the ride," the elaboration can broaden. By this time, we hope, the story line itself has begun to ensure participation by means of its own tension. The resultant anticipatory torque now makes it possible for the preacher to delay, even temporarily detour, the movement of the story. Such timing is possible *after* everyone is *inside*. To hint *ahead of time* is to invite listeners to stray.

Lateral Movement

We return now to the matter of the relative distance between preacher and text for a fairly simple observation. We have noted already that sometimes the preacher is *inside the character*, sometimes *inside the story*, and sometimes further distanced, such as when *talking about the story* or *talking with the listeners*. I call this almost infinite variety of distances *lateral movement*. Except for the unusual biblical story that can be handled almost exclusively *inside* (we called it *running the story*), most of the time a story's forward motion also will include our moving "sideways." This may appear confusing, but actually it is quite natural. We do it in ordinary conversation all the time, such as when relating yesterday's event to a friend. It serves to break the monotony of ordinary discourse.

It becomes confusing *only when it is not cued*. Often the voice gives the cue (which of course is impossible to convey through a manuscript), or, as we noted, the eyes. But it needs to be cued. For example, after I had finished the biblical story proper and moved to editorial comment *about* the story, my bridge sentence was "Well, I must say—I think they've got a point, don't you?" Perhaps it seems as though the words "well, I must say" are wasted. But note what would have happened if I had followed "and get out of here" with "I think they've got a point." It would be altogether too abrupt; folks need time to absorb the lateral shift. Likewise, the phrase "Jesus sees their shock, and says" is a similar cue.

Without such aids, we are left with an experience similar to hearing small children relate last night's movie, and we are not sure whether their laugh is part of the story line or is what they did at the movie or is what they are doing now. With proper cues, lateral movement provides helpful variety of presentation.

Questioning the Text

Unless you question the biblical text and even the teller, this sermon will lose its torque. Beyond the requirement of this sermon, the process of questioning the text has other far-reaching consequences. As we observed earlier, there comes great relief for many people when a preacher "dares" to ask what they have always wanted to ask. Moreover, there are many in most congregations who are close to illiterate about the Bible who can be helped by this procedure. Certainly, one defense against having to ever read the Bible is the presumed attitude that people who *have* read it are precisely those who do *not* question it. This misplaced "respect" has contributed to the next generation's ignorance—at least I have found it so in congregations I have served. After all, if you don't read it, you won't know what you ought to believe and don't. My experience is that sermons that include such questioning are the ones that tend to draw the greatest amount of substantive comments after the service.

At the same time, it is important to provide hints that finally there will be a way out of the dilemma, even if not presently evident. That is why I did not wait long before asking, "*Why* on earth would Jesus . . . ?" If a congregation came to believe that we were out to destroy the biblical witness, they would have reason for concern indeed. Hence the obvious: If you cannot find a way out, do not use the text. I once thought that such a statement as this would not need to be made, but now with such broad acceptance of the lectionary, I think it ought to be said.

The lectionary provides a good number of texts we likely would not choose otherwise. I have had preachers say to me, "Well, my job is not to agree with it; my job is to preach it." In several respects this is a faithful kind of affirmation. After all, one of the benefits of the lectionary is to keep us from our using our favorite texts over and over again. *And* it is clear to me that there are numerous theological positions to be found in the Scriptures. Should we not admit we do not agree "but this is our text for today"? In terms of our present discussion, I think such an approach is destructive. The sermon must find a way out of the apparent dilemma.

Narrative Norms

Differences Between Dialogue and Acting

Twice before in this book I have noted with alarm the problem of crossing the line from narrative to dramatic art. When a preacher is inside the flow of a story, it is natural to include actual spoken lines, from the text itself or imagined. Typically, they are surrounded with "She said to him" and "He quickly responded." Occasionally (such as in that powerful dialogue between elder brother and father), the "they all said's" become awkward and unnecessary. "Didn't you agree to work for a denarius?" "Well, yes, of course, but . . . " Such handling of a text can be powerful. One set of spoken lines is fine, maybe two, but then trouble happens if an editorial "he said" does not occur. The listeners begin to worry that you are about to move on stage, and most of us are not qualified to do so credibly.

It is one thing to read or speak interpretatively; it is another to act out a part. You recall how difficult it was to believe the youth next door was really Hamlet in the school play. You knew too much, and the young actor knew too little, to allow the "willing suspension of disbelief" to happen. So you had trouble getting into the flow of the action; you were watching the kid next door.

The same thing happens when a student in preaching lab begins the sermon with "Good morning. My name is Martha, and I'm a friend of Jesus." Under my breath I say, "Well, we'll just see." And see I do, because I watch to see if the posture seems correct, and I listen for proper tone of voice. I do everything but listen to what is being said. (Which is just as well, because often I would hear a pretty incredible subjectivized rendering of the text.) Do you recall those dialogue sermons of a few years ago, in which the sermon was "interrupted" by a listener? The rest was a play, not a sermon.

Whenever listeners move back to watch, they do not lean forward to hear. They *transcend* instead of *participate*.

The Use of Ambiguity Within "Suspended" Sermons

We have observed already that the moment of suspension (in this presently considered type of preaching) occurs at a "dead end," when the biblical story apparently cannot find resolution within itself. Obviously, the story line is at a point of ambiguity. Likewise, *wherever* it is that the preacher goes for help *must begin* also with some sense of ambiguity. One ought not move from dead end to quick fix. In the case of this sermon, it was the prior story in Matthew, so matters were easy. But suppose I had turned to the writings of Paul? It could work if the connecting line said something like "Paul had this same problem" (which is how Keck negotiated his move to Paul). But if the move were to an admonition of Paul's, the connection misses its hold.

So, for example, imagine we are at the moment of suspension with my final phrase, "otherwise, I just don't understand." "But Paul reminds all of us who think we have a lot coming: 'All have sinned and fall short of the glory of God.' " Such a transition just won't work because it suggests by its form that the question that prompted the suspension was not really valid. If that had been the case, we wouldn't have needed the suspension to begin with.

Negotiating the return to the central story is a bit different, yet fairly easy to grasp. The flashback that provides resolution obviously has some kind of closure (that's why we went there to begin with). Yet that closure is more evoked than explained. But it *has* turned the corner we were needing. The key here is to then move back to the central story, but not in summary fashion: "So now we see clearly what we are called to do." No, that won't do. One moves back to the central story at a point slightly prior to the place where one left it. In the case of this sermon I moved on the previous chapter's negative note, "cheated," and then noted that we never compare ourselves with those who have done more, and so on. The issue here is that, finally, we want the resolution internal to the central story, not tacked on.

Titles and Their Participation in Narrativity

If titles somehow are to participate in the spirit of narrativity, they must not be reduced to static topical phrases. I see lots of sermon titles that remind me that I will not need to attend Sunday's service because I now know what the preacher is going to say (presuming for the moment that the sermon is the only reason for going). At most, titles can cue, but they must not let the cat out of the bag. *The best titles I know are those that in some peculiar way participate both in the establishing of the conflict and in its resolution.*

There are no guarantees that one's intention will be matched by comparable result, but I know what I hoped would happen with the use of the title of this sermon. First, I wanted a line that would disclose nothing thematic to readers *prior* to the sermon being preached. If any guessed my text by the reading of the title, I would be disappointed. Next, I wanted a title that would participate in the conflict. "Who could ask for anything more?" Well, *they* could—and did. Then, I wanted a title that in a single line somehow encapsulated the proclamatory aim of the sermon. If listeners happened to read the line while folding the bulletin after the service, would it evoke the sermon? That I thought it might is evidenced by my use of it as the closing sentence of the sermon. And in the case of this particular title, I hoped that whenever the television commercial happened again, then perhaps so would the sermon.

How to find titles for which one hopes this much could take a chapter in itself. Here, I make several brief suggestions. First, keep looking at advertising; ad writers know something about double entendres that can be helpful. Second, find a synonym for a central term in the sermon (generally a secular term for a sacred one), then imagine another context where that second term is utilized and try to recall a phrase associated with it there. For example (although I never had a sermon for this title, and now it's too late), there once was a Pepsi commercial theme sentence that read, "For those who think young." Now, that line "belongs" to Jesus' word about becoming as a little child. In this case the title presented itself to me rather than the other way around, but the principle can be seen nonetheless. The textual term *child* can be replaced with *young*. In a youth culture like ours there are numerous phrases about being youthful. You start snooping around advertising, pithy one-liners, art forms such as poetry, music, and drama, and your own mental resources. You are looking for a word or phrase that (1) is thoroughly associated with a different context altogether and (2) happens to name precisely what you are attempting to do in the sermon.

Now, finding a title candidate is not the end of the matter. The title must really *fit* the sermon, by which I mean fit the sermon's core, not some peripheral or passing matter within it. Moreover, at best the title needs to state the sermon's aim in a positive rather than negative manner. The key is to name the sermonic resolution without it appearing so before the sermon is presented. Finally, "clever" is not the last word. Titles can be so conspicuous as to draw attention away from the sermon. As is true throughout the sermon itself, if the most that can be said is "Now wasn't that clever," listeners draw back to watch. After all, *cleverness* that is noticed is not really clever. Our role as preachers is not to do what obviously is a fine piece of work. Our role is to effect an evocation.

So far we have considered *running the story, delaying the story,* and *suspending the story.* We now turn to the last design to be discussed: *alternating the story.*

Alternating the Story

This option in narrative sermonic design features the recurring movement of the sermon from inside to outside the biblical story. Because more transitions are involved than in the previously discussed options, it is a bit more complicated, if it is to be done well.

In this sermon Dr. Fred Craddock will start outside the text and then move inside. This type of narrative sermon could proceed the other way around—inside first, then outside. One's choosing is dependent upon the particular text and situation. I think that very quickly it will become clear why he began outside. But the key here is in the *multiple* shifts or transitions between the text and other sermon material.

Listen, then, for our preacher, Dr. Fred B. Craddock *alternating the story.*

(Please read out loud.)

"Praying Through Clenched Teeth"
by
Fred B. Craddock

For I would have you know, brethren, that the gospel which was preached by me is not man's gospel. For I did not receive it from man, nor was I taught it, but it came through a revelation of Jesus Christ. For you have heard of my former life in Judaism, how I persecuted the church of God violently and tried to destroy it; and I advanced in Judaism beyond many of my own age among my people, so extremely zealous was I for the traditions of my fathers. But when he who had set me apart before I was born, and had called me through his grace, was pleased to reveal his Son to me, in order that I might preach him among the Gentiles, I did not confer with flesh and blood, nor did I go up to Jerusalem to those who were apostles before me, but I went away into Arabia; and again I returned to Damascus. Then after three years I went up to Jerusalem to visit Cephas, and remained with him fifteen days. But I saw none of the other apostles except James the Lord's brother. (In what I am writing to you, before God, I do not lie!) Then I went into the regions of Syria and Cilicia. And I was still not known by sight to the churches of Christ in Judea; they only heard it said, "He who once persecuted us is now preaching the faith he once tried to destroy." And they glorified God because of me. (Galatians 1:11-24)

I am going to say a word, and the moment I say the word I want you to see a face, to recall a face and a name, someone who comes to your mind when I say the word. Are you ready? The word is "bitter." Bitter. Do you see a face? I see a face. I see the face of a farmer in western Oklahoma, riding a mortgaged tractor, burning gasoline purchased on credit, moving across rented land, rearranging the dust. Bitter.

Do you see a face? I see the face of a woman forty-seven years old. She sits out on a hillside, drawn and confused under a green canopy furnished by the mortuary. She is banked on all sides by flowers sprinkled with cards: "You have our condolences." Bitter.

Do you see a face? I see the face of a man who runs a small grocery store. His father ran the store in that neighborhood for twenty years, and he is now in his twelfth year there. The grocery doesn't make much profit, but it keeps the family together. It's a business. There are no customers in the store now, and the grocer stands in the doorway with his apron rolled up around his waist, looking across the street where workmen are completing a supermarket. Bitter.

I see the face of a young couple. They seem to be about nineteen. They are standing in the airport terminal, holding hands so tight their knuckles are white. She's pregnant; he's dressed in military green. They are not talking, just standing and looking at each other. The loudspeaker comes on: "Flight 392 now loading at Gate 22, yellow concourse, all aboard for San Francisco." He slowly moves toward the gate; she stands there alone. Bitter.

Do you see a face? A young minister in a small town, in a cracker box of a house they call a parsonage. He lives there with his wife and small child. It's Saturday morning. There is a knock at the door. He answers, and there standing before him on the porch is the chairman of his church board, who is also the president of the local bank, and also the owner of most of the land round about. The man has in his hands a small television. It is an old television, small screen, black and white. It's badly scarred and one of the knobs is off. He says, "My wife and I got one of those new twenty-five-inch color sets, but they didn't want to take this one on a trade, so I just said to myself, "Well, we'll just give it to the minister. That's probably the reason our ministers don't stay any longer than they do, we don't do enough nice things for them." The young minister looks up, tries to smile and say thanks. But I want you to see his face. Bitter.

Will you look at one other face? His name is Saul, Saul of Tarsus. We call him Paul. He was young and intelligent, committed to the traditions of his fathers, strong and zealous for his nation and for his religion, outstripping, he says, all of his classmates in his zeal for his people. While he pursues his own convictions, there develops within the bosom of Judaism a new group called Nazarenes, followers of Jesus. They seemed at first to pose no threat; after all, Judaism had long been broadly liberal and had tolerated within her house of faith a number of groups such as Pharisees and Sadducees and Essenes and Zealots, so why not Nazarenes? As long as they continue in the temple and in the synagogue, there's no problem.

But before long, among these new Christians a different sound is heard. Some of the young radicals are beginning to say that Christianity is not just for the Jews but for anyone who believes in Jesus Christ. Such was the preaching of Stephen and Philip and others; it doesn't really matter if your background is Jewish as long as you trust in God and believe in Jesus Christ. This startling word strikes the ear of young Saul. "What do they mean, it doesn't matter? It does matter! It is the most important matter. No young preacher can stand up and say that thousands of years of mistreatment and exile and burden, of trying to be true to God, of struggling to be his people and keep the candle of faith burning in a dark and pagan world mean nothing. What does he mean, it doesn't matter to have your gabardine spat upon, and to be made fun of because you are different? Of course, it matters!"

Imagine yourself the only child of your parents, but when you are seventeen years old, they adopt a seventeen-year-old brother for you. When you are both eighteen, your father says at breakfast one morning: "I have just had the lawyer draw up the papers. I am leaving the family business to our *two* sons." How do you feel? "This other fellow just got here. He's not really a true son. Where was he when I was mowing the lawn, cleaning the room, trying to pass the ninth grade, and being refused the family car on Friday nights? And now that I'm eighteen, I suddenly have this brother out of nowhere, and he is to share equally?" How would you feel? Would you be saying, "Isn't my father generous?" Not likely.

Then imagine how the young Saul feels. Generations and generations and generations of being the people of God, and now someone in the name of Jesus of Nazareth gets this strange opinion that it doesn't matter anymore, that Jews and Gentiles are alike. You must sense how Saul feels. All your family and national traditions, all that you have ever known and believed, now erased completely from the board? Every moment in school, every belief held dear, every job toward which your life is pointed, now meaningless? Everything that grandfather and father and now you believed, gone? Of course, he resolves to stop it. The dark cloud of his brooding bitterness forms a tornado funnel over that small church, and he strikes it, seeking to end it. In the name of his fathers, in the name of his country, in the name of God, yes.

Now, why does he do this? Why is he so bitter at this announcement of the universal embrace of all people in the name of God? Do you know what I believe? I believe he is bitter and disturbed because he is at war with himself over this very matter. And anyone at war with himself will make casualties even out of friends and loved ones. He is himself uncertain, and it is the uncertain person who becomes a persecutor, until like a wounded animal he lies in the sand near Damascus, waiting for the uplifted stroke of a God whom he thinks he serves.

But Paul knows his is a God who loves all creation. He knows; surely he knows. Saul has read his Bible. He has read that marvelous book of Ruth, in which the ancestress of David is shamelessly presented as a Moabite woman. Certainly, God loves other peoples. He has read the book of Jonah and the expressed love of God for people that Jonah himself does not love. Paul has read the book of Isaiah and the marvelous vision of the house of God into which all nations flow. It is in his Bible. Then what's his problem? His problem is the same problem you and I have had sometimes. It's one thing to know something; it's another thing to *know* it. He knows it and he does not know it, and the battle that is fought between knowing and really knowing is fierce. It is sometimes called the struggle from head to heart. I know that the longest trip we ever make is the trip from head to heart, from knowing to knowing, and until that trip is complete, we are in great pain. We might even lash out at others.

Do you know anyone bitter like this; bitter that what they are fighting is what they know is right? Trapped in that impossible battle of trying to stop the inevitable triumph of the truth? Do you know anyone lashing out in criticism and hatred and violence against a person or against a group that represents the humane and caring and Christian way? If you do, how do you respond? Hopefully you do not react to bitterness with bitterness. We certainly have learned that such is a futile and fruitless endeavor, just as I hope we have learned we do not fight prejudice with prejudice. A few years ago, many of us found ourselves more prejudiced against prejudiced people than the prejudiced people were prejudiced. Then how do we respond?

Let me tell you a story. A family is out for a drive on a Sunday afternoon. It is a pleasant afternoon, and they relax at a leisurely pace down the highway. Suddenly the two children begin to beat their father in the back: "Daddy, Daddy, stop the car! Stop the car! There's a kitten back there on the side of the road!" The father says, "So there's a kitten on the side of the road. We're having a drive." "But Daddy, you must stop and pick it up." "I don't have to stop and pick it up." "But Daddy, if you don't, it will die." "Well, then it will have to die. We don't have room for another animal. We have a zoo already at the house. No more animals." "But Daddy, are you going to just let it die?" "Be quiet, children; we're trying to have a pleasant drive." "We never thought our Daddy would be so mean and cruel as to let a kitten die." Finally the mother turns to her husband and says, "Dear, you'll have to stop." He turns the car around, returns to the spot and pulls off to the side of the road. "You kids stay in the car. I'll see about it." He goes out to pick up the little kitten. The poor creature is just skin and bones, sore-eyed, and full of fleas; but when he reaches down to pick it up, with its last bit of energy the kitten bristles, baring tooth and claw. Sssst! He picks up the kitten by the loose skin at the neck, brings it over to the car and says, "Don't touch it; it's probably got leprosy." Back home they go. When they get to the house the children give the kitten several baths, about a gallon of warm milk, and intercede: "Can we let it stay in the house just tonight? Tomorrow we'll fix a place in the garage." The father says, "Sure, take my bedroom; the whole house is already a zoo." They fix a comfortable bed, fit for a pharaoh. Several weeks pass. Then one day the father walks in, feels something rub against his leg, looks down, and there is a cat. He reaches down toward the cat, carefully checking to see that no one is watching. When the cat sees his hand, it does not bare its claws and hiss; instead it arches its back to receive a caress. Is that the same cat? Is that the same cat? No. It's not the same as that frightened, hurt, hissing kitten on the side of the road. Of course not. And you know as well as I what makes the difference.

Not too long ago God reached out his hand to bless me and my family. When he did, I looked at his hand; it was covered with scratches. Such is the hand of love, extended to those who are bitter.

Let us look more closely at this sermon, attempting to discern how the preacher enabled our experience.

Running Commentary

I am going to say a word, and the moment I say the word I want you to see a face, to recall a face and a name, someone who comes to your mind when I say the word. Are you ready? The word is "bitter." Bitter. Do you see a face? I see a face. I see the face of a farmer in western Oklahoma, riding a mortgaged tractor, burning gasoline purchased on credit, moving across rented land, rearranging the dust. Bitter.

The sermon begins without reference to the text. Fred Craddock merely asks of us a simple request. Before we can settle on a face, he gives us one. Note that his entire reference to the farmer is handled in a single sentence. His quick evocation is managed through two devices: first, the use of vivid, active verbs—"riding," "burning," "moving" and "rearranging"; and, second, by the powerful word picture "rearranging the dust." I believe it would be difficult to overestimate the power this one phrase has to rivet the attention of the listeners for what is to follow. Whose mind can stray after that?

Do you see a face? I see the face of a woman forty-seven years old. She sits out on a hillside, drawn and confused under a green canopy furnished by the mortuary. She is banked on all sides by flowers sprinkled with cards: "You have our condolences." Bitter.

Craddock gives us another quick scene. The description is a bit more enfleshed, taking three sentences to accomplish. Twice now the scene is framed by a single word: "bitter." The wording of the card evokes more than it says and reminds us that the quickest route to the universal is through the particular.

Do you see a face? I see the face of a man who runs a small grocery store. His father ran the store in that neighborhood for twenty years, and he is now in his twelfth year there. The grocery doesn't make much profit, but it keeps the family together. It's a business. There are no customers in the store now, and the grocer stands in the doorway with his apron rolled up around his waist, looking across the street where workmen are completing a supermarket. Bitter.

Have you noticed that in each succeeding scene the details are becoming fuller, with this scene requiring five sentences?

We ought to observe, also, that Craddock is doing something else here without our noticing. He is cultivating our empathy with those who are bitter. We will need this attitude when he gets to Paul a little later. Is this the reason he began with several contemporary scenes prior to the biblical text, rather than the other way around?

I see the face of a young couple. They seem to be about nineteen. They are standing in the airport terminal, holding hands so tight their knuckles are white. She's pregnant; he's dressed in military green. They are not talking, just standing and looking at each other. The loudspeaker comes on: "Flight 392 now loading at Gate 22, yellow concourse, all aboard for San Francisco." He slowly moves toward the gate; she stands there alone. Bitter.

With this airport scene Craddock has now given us four pictures, with the description growing from one to three to five to now seven sentences. (The next will take eleven.) It is surely no accident. Had the word pictures been reversed in the amount of detail given, listeners might become nervous about the introduction of a new scene.

With this couple at the airport, Craddock does not tell us in generalized terms about the state of their souls or current emotional health; he shows us white knuckles. We do the rest.

Do you see a face? A young minister in a small town, in a cracker box of a house they call a parsonage. He lives there with his wife and small child. It's Saturday morning. There is a knock at the door. He answers, and there standing before him on the porch is the chairman of his church board, who is also the president of the local bank, and also the owner of most of the land round about. The man has in his hands a small television. It is an old television, small screen, black and white. It's badly scarred and one of the knobs is off. He says: "My wife and I got one of those new twenty-five-inch color sets, but they didn't want to take this one on a trade, so I just

*said to myself, "Well, we'll just give it to the minister.
That's probably the reason our ministers don't stay any
longer than they do, we don't do enough nice things for
them." The young minster looks up, tries to smile and say
thanks. But I want you to see his face. Bitter.*

We come now to the most complicated of the several
vignettes. The fact that this scene is that of a parsonage
makes me wonder if this sermon was originally presented
to a worship gathering of clergy. I do not know if this is the
case, but it does raise an important issue, which is that the
torque of increased suspense or anticipation (as Craddock
himself puts it) can be enhanced by the arrangement of
various sequential vignettes. It always makes good sense
not only to enhance the complication through increased
detail but also to move toward the ever-close-at-hand.
Knowing Craddock's fine homiletical intuitions makes me
think the congregation knew something about cracker
boxes called parsonages, one way or another.

We need to observe also the way Craddock uses syntax
to embody the content of his speaking. A closer look at the
sentence structure in this paragraph reveals that with a
couple of exceptions all the sentences are simple, direct,
and short—"It's Saturday morning"—except for the
description of or speech by the banker. Note that the
sentence that describes how his wealth and position go on
and on is presented by a sentence that goes on and on.

*Will you look at one other face? His name is Saul, Saul
of Tarsus. We call him Paul. He was young and
intelligent, committed to the traditions of his fathers,
strong and zealous for his nation and for his religion,
outstripping, he says, all of his classmates in his zeal for
his people. While he pursues his own convictions, there
develops within the bosom of Judaism a new group
called Nazarenes, followers of Jesus. They seemed at first
to pose no threat; after all, Judaism had long been
broadly liberal and had tolerated within her house of
faith a number of groups such as Pharisees and
Sadducees and Essenes and Zealots, so why not*

Nazarenes? As long as they continue in the temple and in the synagogue, there's no problem.

Finally, we arrive at the depiction of Saul. Some of the listeners have already forgotten the text, which is exactly what is required. Had Craddock reversed the order by first presenting this word picture of Saul, we would have brought all our stereotypes of Saul along with us. We all know that stupid anger of Saul, born of his early refusal to accept Christ. Craddock wants us to approach Saul in a different mood, hence the four vignettes. Now we are ready to encounter the scene with empathy.

In bringing us to Saul, our preacher does not actually go to the text of the sermon but *through* the text to the story behind the story. Both preachers and listeners have trouble getting behind any resolution. In the text Paul is a Christian; before that he was a persecutor of the church. Craddock takes us to a time prior even to that, when Saul is a loyal, patriotic, and faithful Jew. As he says, "No problem."

> *But before long, among these new Christians a different sound is heard. Some of the young radicals are beginning to say that Christianity is not just for the Jews but for anyone who believes in Jesus Christ. Such was the preaching of Stephen and Philip and others; it doesn't really matter if your background is Jewish as long as you trust in God and believe in Jesus Christ. This startling word strikes the ear of young Saul. "What do they mean, it doesn't matter? It does matter! It is the most important matter. No young preacher can stand up and say that thousands of years of mistreatment and exile and burden, of trying to be true to God, of struggling to be his people and keep the candle of faith burning in a dark and pagan world mean nothing. What does he mean, it doesn't matter to have your gabardine spat upon, and to be made fun of because you are different? Of course, it matters!"*

Yet there *is* a problem, and our preacher presents it in a manner totally sympathetic to Saul's conservative and deeply held commitments. Contrast that with those who lack such abiding loyalty and patriotic faithfulness. They are presented both as "young" and "radical." Craddock puts well-chosen words to their character, that they claim being a Jew "doesn't matter." He could have said their view is that "salvation is predicated on deeper matters than racial purity or theological orthodoxy." No, they are characterized as believing it "doesn't matter." Now, we all know what to think of anyone who says something "doesn't matter." Through such crisp value-laden descriptions all of us must take the side of Saul. More important, we are provided here with an in-depth analysis of Saul's motivation, which exists prior to behavior Craddock knows we will not approve. He gives us *good* reasons for *bad* actions and keeps the sermonic tension alive. When given the choice between the "candle of faith" and the "dark and pagan world," we know where to stand.

Imagine yourself the only child of your parents, but when you are seventeen years old, they adopt a seventeen-year-old brother for you. When you are both eighteen, your father says at breakfast one morning "I have just had the lawyer draw up the papers. I am leaving the family business to our two sons." How do you feel? "This other fellow just got here. He's not really a true son. Where was he when I was mowing the lawn, cleaning the room, trying to pass the ninth grade, and being refused the family car on Friday nights? And now that I'm eighteen, I suddenly have this brother out of nowhere, and he is to share equally?" How would you feel? Would you be saying, "Isn't my father generous?" Not likely.

But just in case we don't know where to stand—and there might be some anti-Saul prejudice left by this time—Craddock jumps out of the biblical setting and into our world. He tells a parallel story, freely invented. Note how he has utilized in a family setting several of the ingredients of the biblical issue. The adopted son is new to the scene, hasn't paid the price of family membership, hasn't even had occasion to experience negative rebuke. Moreover, Craddock's choice of a family portrait has the result of our imaging Saul's setting as family, too. By now our logical and emotional commitments have to be solidly in place.

Then imagine how the young Saul feels. Generations and generations and generations of being the people of God, and now someone in the name of Jesus of Nazareth gets this strange opinion that it doesn't matter anymore, that Jews and Gentiles are alike. You must sense how Saul feels. All your family and national traditions, all that you have ever known and believed, now erased completely from the board? Every moment in school, every belief held dear, every job toward which your life is pointed, now meaningless? Everything that grandfather and father and now you believed, gone? Of course, he resolves to stop it. The dark cloud of his brooding bitterness forms a tornado funnel over that small church, and he strikes it, seeking to end it. In the name of his fathers, in the name of his country, in the name of God, yes.

With our sentiments in order, the sermonic flow now alternates back to the biblical setting. Note how our preacher picks up on the family image as he restates the case for Saul. He could have used family imagery in a prior rendering, but he waited until the contemporary story was told.

Only now, after all is clear, does Craddock allow us to consider Saul's resultant behavior of persecution. And even as he presents it, the beginning phrase is "Of course."

Note how in this summary, even repetition, of the soundness of Saul's convictions—indeed, now our own—the preacher switches the pronoun from "his" to "your." Note, too, that Craddock does not use any form of the term *persecution*—even though it occurs in the scripture lesson. In previous sections things "mattered" to Saul; now he acts. He acts because everything is at stake—and in the name of everything dear.

Now, why does he do this? Why is he so bitter at this announcement of the universal embrace of all people in the name of God? Do you know what I believe? I believe he is bitter and disturbed because he is at war with himself over this very matter. And anyone at war with himself will make casualties even out of friends and loved ones. He is himself uncertain, and it is the uncertain person who becomes a persecutor, until like a wounded animal he lies in the sand near Damascus, waiting for the uplifted stroke of a God whom he thinks he serves.

We have to be shocked that after all this build-up defending Saul's convictions and resultant actions, we now should have disclosed to us the decisive claim that those reasons do not constitute the whole issue. In just four sentences Craddock shifts everything and provides the decisive turn of the sermon. But why didn't the preacher just say so to begin with? Why this elaborate defense of Saul, including the use of a contemporary story and then a return to the biblical context for a further summary? The reason is simple: Had he told us earlier, we would not have experienced its truth. Certainly, we might have *believed* it, but it would not have been *real* for us. Had we been told earlier that Saul had this interior problem, the issue would have remained flat. We would have observed it and remained outside. But this way we are inside the problem.

But Paul knows his is a God who loves all creation. He knows; surely he knows. Saul has read his Bible. He has read that marvelous book of Ruth, in which the ancestress of David is shamelessly presented as a Moabite woman. Certainly, God loves other peoples. He has read the book of Jonah and the expressed love of God for people that Jonah himself does not love. Paul has read the book of Isaiah and the marvelous vision of the house of God into which all nations flow. It is in his Bible. Then what's his problem? His problem is the same problem you and I have had sometimes. It's one thing to know something; it's another thing to know *it. He knows it and he does not know it, and the battle that is fought between knowing and really knowing is fierce. It is sometimes called the struggle from head to heart. I know that the longest trip we ever make is the trip from head to heart, from knowing to knowing, and until that trip is complete, we are in great pain. We might even lash out at others.*

Craddock is not through with making things rich in complication. He now appears to leave us hanging regarding his claim about the internal war inside Saul to reveal another part of the truth Saul knew. But this just now revealed part of Saul—that he knew God's care for all people—is what provides the other pole of his dilemmratic situation.

Craddock could have revealed this side of Saul immediately preceding his announcement about the internal war, and that method certainly is feasible. He chose to delay it until after the decisive turn, I believe, in order to maximize our situational involvement. Note how his explanation about the two kinds of knowing involve reference to us as well as Saul. As Craddock put it, "His problem is the same problem you and I have had sometimes." We have here a double-turn sermon—first the war within, and then the two kinds of knowing. By the time the preacher has revealed the dynamics of this complicated situation, we receive a shock of recognition as he notes that in *our* pain "We might even lash out at others."

Do you know anyone bitter like this; bitter that what they are fighting is what they know is right? Trapped in that impossible battle of trying to stop the inevitable triumph of the truth? Do you know anyone lashing out in criticism and hatred and violence against a person or against a group that represents the humane and caring and Christian way? If you do, how do you respond? Hopefully you do not react to bitterness with bitterness. We certainly have learned that such is a futile and fruitless endeavor, just as I hope we have learned we do not fight prejudice with prejudice. A few years ago, many of us found ourselves more prejudiced against prejudiced people than the prejudiced people were prejudiced. Then how do we respond?

As Craddock shifts once again from biblical to contemporary context, it will be instructive to note how he negotiates the move. Actually, he began the shift a few lines before the manuscript's new paragraph. Recall that he noted how Saul's problem is our problem. He began mixing pronouns repeatedly—from "his" to "our," and so forth. The last sentence referred to us—yet remained in the biblical context. Now the first sentence of the new paragraph lands us in the here and now by his asking if we "know anyone . . . " Otherwise put, the unresolved, problematic issue is the glue for transition. Contrast that with the all-too-typical method that buttons down the biblical portion with the closure of summary and then tries to open things up with such a phrase as "Now, the same thing is true for us today," in which case you have to start over again at the top.

Let me tell you a story. A family is out for a drive on a Sunday afternoon. It is a pleasant afternoon, and they relax at a leisurely pace down the highway. Suddenly the two children begin to beat their father in the back: "Daddy, Daddy, stop the car! Stop the car! There's a kitten back there on the side of the road!" The father says, "So there's a kitten on the side of the road. We're having a drive." "But Daddy, you must stop and pick it up." "I don't have to stop and pick it up." "But Daddy, if you don't, it will die." "Well, then it will have to die. We don't have room for another animal. We have a zoo already at the house. No more animals." "But Daddy, are you going to just let it die?" "Be quiet, children; we're trying to have a pleasant drive." "We never thought our Daddy would be so mean and cruel as to let a kitten die." Finally the mother turns to her husband and says, "Dear, you'll have to stop." He turns the car around, returns to the spot and pulls off to the side of the

*road. "You kids stay in the car. I'll see about it." He goes
out to pick up the little kitten. The poor creature is just
skin and bones, sore-eyed, and full of fleas; but when he
reaches down to pick it up, with its last bit of energy the
kitten bristles, baring tooth and claw. Sssst! He picks up
the kitten by the loose skin at the neck, brings it over to
the car and says, "Don't touch it; it's probably got
leprosy." Back home they go. When they get to the house
the children give the kitten several baths, about a gallon
of warm milk, and intercede: "Can we let it stay in the
house just tonight? Tomorrow we'll fix a place in the
garage." The father says, "Sure, take my bedroom; the
whole house is already a zoo." They fix a comfortable
bed, fit for a pharaoh. Several weeks pass. Then one day
the father walks in, feels something rub against his leg,
looks down, and there is a cat. He reaches down toward
the cat, carefully checking to see that no one is watching.
When the cat sees his hand, it does not bare its claws and
hiss; instead it arches its back to receive a caress. Is that
the same cat? Is that the same cat? No. It's not the same as
that frightened, hurt, hissing kitten on the side of the
road. Of course not. And you know as well as I what
makes the difference.*

The preacher has just asked us a direct question: "Then
how do we respond?" But instead of talking with us about
proper response, he now launches into another freely
invented story. Surely the story somehow will answer his
question. We hope so. And so it is that we are confronted
with a critical homiletical issue, namely the relation of
trust to sermonic transition. Clearly this is a moment when
the listeners might become disengaged. For them to stay
with the sermon requires their confidence that indeed the
preacher will not let them down. If the listeners do not
trust the preacher (born perhaps of previous disappoint-
ments at such critical moments), they will not have the
patience or energy to continue. In this case the preacher,
through graphic description of human nature and clear
focus and direction, has no problem. His previous stories

have borne fruit powerfully. So the listeners wait with eager anticipation to see how he will do it. *With trust,* such shifts result in powerful engagement; *without trust,* such shifts result in disengagement.

There is another surprise in the way Craddock finishes this sermon—unless, of course, you have heard him preach a number of times. Recall that the previous paragraph ended with the question "Then how do we respond?" Were Craddock the typical preacher, one might get nervous that the good news of the gospel might not get named. After all, when a preacher asks how we should respond, typically the gospel has already been announced, and the question has to do with proper response—or, the gospel has been neglected altogether, and the sermon is going to be another self-help admonition. Otherwise put, the *usual* shape of a sermon involves a movement from the indicative of the gospel to the imperative of its claim. And Craddock is asking what our response should be. Note, however, that *here* the usual shape is *in the story* rather than in the sermon. That is, Craddock asks about response and then tells a story that has both good news and response together. The story forces us momentarily to move behind the question of response to that which makes response possible. In so doing, the listener is caught off guard. The good news happens while we are not looking, which empowers it. To be sure, we had a hint about the good news during that section of the sermon when Saul was described as knowing the God who loves all people. Now, through the kitten story, the good news is explicitly evoked. The cat is different—not at all the cat that hissed on the road. "And you know as well as I what makes the difference." In short, Craddock asked about our response, while the story really announces what makes response possible.

Not too long ago God reached out his hand to bless me and my family. When he did, I looked at his hand; it was covered with scratches. Such is the hand of love, extended to those who are bitter.

Craddock wants the matter closer still and moves from cat to autobiography in an imaginative reprise to the good news.

By the way, the title of this sermon made me think this was to be a message about prayer. I guess not. Or is it?

Narrative Capabilities, Techniques, and Norms

Fred Craddock's sermon provides a wonderful opportunity to name a number of narrative procedures and techniques. As with the sermons by Dennis Willis, Leander Keck, and myself, they will be grouped under the categories of capabilities, techniques, and norms.

Narrative Capabilities

Multiple Levels of Communication

The narrative shape of a sermon provides a natural opportunity for multiple levels or forms of communication, and Craddock's preaching provides a fine occasion to experience them.

Perhaps you have observed the fairly narrow parameters that seem to apply in formal discourse. When a lecturer is taking the listeners through a labyrinth of technical detail, or an expository-style preacher is working through the process of an extended text, a personal aside, for example, often seems out of place. When a politician is attempting to claim your vote by a rousing affirmation of country, you would not expect a speech to inform. This presumes, of course, that the above speakers are not utilizing narrative form.

The more traditional forms of public speaking have presumed that the shape of address is determined either by the purpose of the speaking *or* by the subject matter being utilized. In one sense this is precisely correct. At another level it is not. *Narrative form presumes that the nature of the speaker-listener event determines the shape of address.* The result is that greater latitude of communicational form possible. Otherwise put, the torque of listener anticipation provides both the "holding power" of attention and the forward thrust of direction, with the possibility of multiple levels of communication occurring within that movement. Perhaps Craddock's sermon can explain the matter more forcefully.

Craddock begins with *conversational dialogue*: "I am going to say a word . . . and . . . I want you to . . ." Notice the intimacy of "I" and "you." Quickly he moves to *portraits* of the farmer, the widow, and the grocery store owner. The fourth word picture of the airport scene adds the element of time ("He slowly moves") and becomes a modern *exodos*. Conversation is added to the parsonage scene for a *episode*. The more extended treatment of Saul includes a brief informational *didactic* history lesson, even spiced with an implied dialogue between Saul and the "young radicals." Communication through the use of *story* occurs several times, such as "Imagine yourself the only child," and "A family is out for a drive." Craddock's in-depth analysis of Saul's internal war prompts the use of *reasoned discourse*, which moves him into third person speech: "And anyone at war with himself . . . " The sermon concludes in story form with an *autobiographical incident*.

How is it possible for him to range so widely in levels or forms of communicational style? The principle of narrative process provides the underlying commonality that can accommodate these various diverse ingredients. Were Craddock to be viewed as a "story preacher" or an "expository preacher," even the image would constrain the available forms of communication. Certainly Craddock often moves episodally in his preaching. Yet underneath Craddock's explicitly episodal style of preaching—and although often more implicit than obvious—lies *narrativity*. And this sermon reveals powerfully the potentialities of the narrative mode.

The Story Behind the Text

When a given sermon text consists essentially of a report, the preacher is often at a loss to know how to handle it homiletically. The expository style of preaching with which I was raised "solved" the problem simply by going through the text verse by verse, phrase by phrase, and word by word. We often gained valuable information that resulted in new meaning—*if* we could stay hooked to the sermon. The assumption seemed to be that interest in such biblical matters was important for any Christian. And indeed it is. A companion assumption was that the first assumption was reason enough to warrant a hearing. And indeed it is not. The narrative mode of preaching adds another reason—that such "valuable information" and the new meaning it prompts is the only route possible for the resolution to the plot's conflict—the only way home.

As a noted New Testament scholar, Fred Craddock is in a good position to understand the power of the biblical witness and the importance of biblical history. He does not, however, rely solely on our Christian virtue as motivation for our hearing. He causes such material to become indispensable to the resolution of the sermonic narrative. Observe how Craddock does it.

The text comes from the first chapter of the letter of Paul to the Galatians. He has elected to center on Paul's reminder to the Galatian churches of his former life within Judaism. The sermon utilizes Paul's own experience to focus on bitterness. Craddock knows we need to understand something about the biblical situation out of which Paul's experience comes. We are going to need a bit of knowledge about the Essenes and Pharisees, as well as such folks as Stephen and Philip. He could have begun with a brief history lesson to prepare us for the sermon. But he doesn't. Instead, he first introduces us to various faces of bitterness and makes Saul his final example. Of course, we now need to know just *why* Saul is bitter, and we need to understand the adequacy of the reasons behind it. The unresolved conflictual nature of bitterness itself provides the rationale for our hearing.

Likewise, that the Bible reveals a God who "loves all creation" is a part of Saul's experience and, more important, is the ground out of which the whole message grows. Note how "problematically" Craddock introduces this section of important information: "He knows; surely he knows."

Actually, there are two levels of narrativity at work here. First of all, the sermon is set in *narrative form*. Second, the indispensable biblical information is inserted in *story form*, which just happens to be rich in metaphorical possibility. The result is that Craddock can mean more than he actually says, leading by implication and evocation. Such a technique not only keeps us on track with where he wants us to go, but it also allows us to become participants in the process. Utilization of the story behind the text is facilitated by the narrative form of the sermon.

Narrative Techniques

Language Use

Craddock cares for the English language and knows how to use it. We have already had occasion in the running commentary to take note of some of his language techniques. For example, we observed the power of his phrase "rearranging the dust." Note that the power of the phrase is occasioned by the use of a verb.

When in English composition class, I thought "being descriptive" meant using a lot of adjectives and adverbs. But typically, the use of a modifier does what the term suggests—it *modifies*. That is, it alters or shapes. Most of us are not greatly impacted by an alteration. We are impacted by a radically new and different image. To do that, one needs the power of nouns and verbs. Moreover, modifiers clutter, complicate the sentence structure, which again tends to dilute the power. They also call attention to the sentence and hence to the speaker.

"Rearranging the dust"—its startling power is not simply due to the fact of utilizing a verb but to the particular verb chosen. I can imagine many of us might have stumbled onto the term "dust," given the fact of the "dust bowl." So we might have come up with "plowing dust." Not bad. But "rearranging the dust"? How could he have thought it up? Must the rest of us simply stand in awe? Probably. And yet, on the other hand, I do believe it is possible for all of us to learn how to learn. We may think the result of our efforts a bit feeble in comparison. But the proper comparison is not with anyone else; the proper comparison is between how we do things now and how we *might* do things. Of course, I do not know for sure how Craddock came up with "rearranging the dust," nor how automatically or quickly. But the distance between "plowing his field" and "rearranging the dust" is not insurmountable. Once the "dust bowl" image comes, the next step is to think of other contexts that utilize the term "dust." (which is how metaphors are born). "Dust" brings us to "house cleaning," which brings us to the self-effacing phrase "Well, I was just rearranging the dust." There you have it. Whether this is the way it happened for Craddock, I do not know. But the principle is nameable. Find another term for the usual one, then find another context for the new term, and then find a phrase associated within that other context. Obviously it won't always work, but powerful phrases generally come from such metaphorical thinking.

A similar principle is at work in Craddock's treatment of the differences between faithful Saul and the "young radicals." Clearly he wanted to "slant" the descriptions so that we could be supportive of Saul. Sometimes such treatment is called the use of "purr words" and "slur words." I call it heavily value-laden language. Instead of a spatial distance, as between plowing a field and cleaning a house, Craddock utilized a temporal distance. He chose words familiar to us in our time and applied them to the biblical characters (as did Keck in his sermon). Moreover, the use of such loaded designations powerfully abbreviates a long paragraph of explanation. And it enables the listeners to participate in the task. After all, engagement in listening is in part having something to do.

Use of Repetition

We had occasion to note the effective use of repetition in Willis's sermon. Its effective use is evident in this sermon as well. Note how the entire sermon hinged on the term "bitter." It will be helpful to notice when he used it and when he did not.

The term was the last word for each of the opening word pictures. It was effective because with each use we had more data to attach to it. At first I was surprised when he didn't use it after the first picture of Saul was presented. My further reflection suggests his *not* using it was not an inadvertent omission. A term like "bitter" has a closure quality to it. It summarizes by evocation. And in the word pictures prior to Saul, there was nothing that could be done—plow and be bitter, grieve and be bitter, get on the plane and be bitter, take the television set and be bitter. But in the case of Saul in his relation with the Christians, there *was* something he could and would do. The matter was not closed but open. To have used the term "bitter" *then* in part would be to close down the sermon just when the preacher wanted to open it up. He chose not to use it for a one-sentence summary. (The term was included in the middle of several discussions, but not as summary evocation.) The term is then used as the closing word of the sermon, but, again, not as summary. The transformation of its reality is named in that closing line: "Such is the hand of love, extended to those who are bitter."

Reprise to the Good News

In the running commentary we reflected on how, toward the close of the sermon, Craddock asked a question about human response and then told a story that, metaphorically, really featured the act of grace that makes response possible. Not content with leaving us with the kitten story, he then added three autobiographical lines. This is a powerful example of the technique of reprise, named in our consideration of the sermon of Dennis Willis. "I looked at his hand; it was covered with scratches" provides precisely the "tag line," the "one more time" technique, that was described earlier. Yet sermonic power is not all that is at stake for Craddock. Those who have often heard him preach will recognize this as one of several methods he utilizes in order to "put the ball in our court" (as we called it earlier). I wouldn't be at all surprised if after he completed the sermon, the liturgist for the occasion stood to "finish" the sermon with something like "I'm sure we are all grateful to Dr. Craddock for this powerful message about how we can live without bitterness and be open to viewing all people as children of God." My guess is that he has had many sermons "completed" in this way or perhaps through someone's closing prayer. The intentions are noble, of course, but behind them lies a different mentality that affects the purpose of our preaching. Most of us have been taught to "close it down," make specific and clear what it is the listeners are supposed to think or be or do. This is all to the point—*except* we have taken such advice to mean *"Do all the work."* When specificity of aim *includes* the further assumption that all action occurs behind the pulpit, then passivity will be experienced in front of the pulpit. Craddock trusts the listeners to hear the specificity and then to handle the behaviors clearly implied. Such is the reason his listeners regularly have come to experience his back—that is, when least expected, Craddock will suddenly turn from the pulpit and walk away. The "dance of the mind" as we scramble to reconstruct that last sentence is vintage Craddock, made possible sometimes through the use of reprise.

Freely Invented Stories

In order to gain listener identification and attitudinal set with the biblical text, Craddock often will utilize a freely invented story. Such is the case with the adopted son story. Sometimes the purpose is to help the listeners know what to do with the message of the text—hence the kitten episode. In both cases he cued the story in advance with such phrases as "Imagine" and "Let me tell you a story." Often the imaginative content is cued by a word *inside* the story, such as within another sermon of his that said, "Down the street where *you* live." Sometimes there is no cue at all, such as "Not too long ago God reached out his hand."

The primary effect of this technique is to enable a fresh look at some reality without the impediment of a prejudiced attitude. Likewise, the relevance of the culturally distant text gets evoked when set in a new frame. All this we have considered already. There is another, perhaps more important, purpose for preachers attempting such freely invented stories. Such recreations will open the mind of the preacher. I suggest their use even if the final result is judged not good enough to be included in the finished sermon. Before the shock of recognition can occur for listeners, it needs to occur for the preacher. Freely invented stories often prompt that shock.

Narrative Norms

Increased Complication

Increasing the opening conflict of any narrative sermon is central, of course, to the process. Most of us have little difficulty discerning its purpose and the ways by which to accomplish it. Seldom, however, do you find it performed with such finely honed skill as here in Craddock's sermon. We called attention to it in the running commentary, and for our sake it now deserves a further look.

With the previous sermon we approached this issue in our consideration of paraphrasing. I suggested the importance of beginning with a tight paraphrase and then moving toward greater elaboration. In this sermon we discover how Craddock embodies this increasing complication through the means of language use.

Not only do his opening word pictures move in description from one to three to five to seven to eleven sentences, but in the fourth scene he also provides action and in the fifth he supplies dialogue. Later in the sermon he is describing Saul, and word choice is his method of complication.

First Saul has a "problem," which becomes a "battle," which is "fierce" enough to cause "great pain"—enough pain that we might "lash out." All this happens in fewer than thirty seconds. Did you notice that not only do the terms move toward greater intensity, they also move from general to specific? Compare "problem" to "lash out." Likewise, the sweep moves from Saul to us.

In all the above-noted matters, Craddock's *manner of speaking* embodies the *content of his speaking*. Naturally, the question is, Beyond deep appreciation, what can we do about it in our own preaching? My assumption is that such language use has become second nature for him. (He might even be a bit amused by our noticing.) In any event, such language use may not be second nature for us. How does one learn how to do such things?

The only way I know to begin learning such things is by reviewing carefully our present work. Don't plan to do it for next Sunday's sermon; instead, examine last Sunday's sermon. This is difficult to do because we are glad to have last Sunday gone.

Nonetheless, I suggest we might dust off that old English composition text, refamiliarize ourselves with its terms, and choose a small section of last Sunday's sermon for examination. (It is not hard to produce a text from an audiorecording.) Look at sentence structure, at the relative weight of modifiers and nouns and verbs, and so on. Assess word choice in the sermon as delivered. In short, examine *how* we formed what it was that we were attempting to accomplish. Were form and content congruent? From our vantage point it may *appear* to come easy for others; we will have to work at it. Yet the development of congruity between *what* we say and *how* we say it will be worth the effort we expend, because our sermons will be empowered.

Here, Craddock's purpose was to increase the complication of the narrative process. His language use successfully accomplished his goal.

Actions, Motives, and Credibility

The narrative sermon's need for complication and the diagnostician's need for in-depth analysis provides a happy confluence of interests at the point of motivation. The need for complication in the narrative sermon process has been underscored repeatedly. It occurs inevitably when the preacher moves behind the simplicity of behavior into the complexity of the world of motivations.

As I suggested in a previous book, the facticity of the prodigal son's behavior, for example, is a simple either-or matter. Either he stays home or he goes away. The question of his motives in desiring to leave home is an altogether different matter. There is no simple single motive to account for his decision. He may not even be aware of some of the dynamics of his choice.

There even is a temporal ebb and flow of motive. Things are fluid, deep, and sometimes ambiguous in terms of values. Hence, the move from behavior to motive is one major way to allow complication of the plot line. Craddock reveals the technique well, particularly in his discussion of why Saul wound up opposing the new Christian movement. And the torque of tension is heightened mightily by his illustration of the adopted son. But there is more here to be learned than effective narrative process.

This complication of plot line—with its snooping exploration of motive—is causing something else to happen. Listeners are attending closely to see how keenly the preacher is doing the diagnostic work. During this time the listeners are making judgments about the preacher's judgments. Does the preacher take analytic shortcuts to quick generalizations about the causes behind human behavior? Given the preacher's understanding about human nature, should you trust the sermon's final claim? Or is this just "preacher talk" from someone who doesn't really know how the world works?

Out of this probing into depth comes *trust*—or *suspicion*.

The listener who is not so sure about the way people are being treated in the sermon will look for reasons to dismiss the message. On the other hand, when listeners begin to believe the preacher apparently knows them better than they know themselves, a kind of communion emerges.

The post-service comment, "You seemed to be talking directly to me today," is an attempt to own the fact of that communion. When communication is this effective, the character of the relationship moves beyond typical speaker-listener categories, and one needs some other word like *intimacy* to fully describe it. No longer is the speaker just "effective"; the speaker becomes *friend*.

I believe that it is because of this kind of communicational depth that listeners were willing to trust Craddock when he said: "Let me tell you a story." Who could say no? Whether or not he would answer the question he had just posed became momentarily moot. Only with such presumed sense of intimacy could he then conclude, "Not too long ago God reached out." Never mind that he gave us no particulars about the experience, except for figurative detail. It *had* to be true, because for us it had already *become true* in his telling.

Postlude

Now that we have thoroughly explored the four sermons, we can more likely imagine how the various narrative preaching designs relate to the three basic preparation issues of focus, turn, and aim.

Note first that the process of choosing from among the design options is determined in part by how the biblical story and the question of focus and turn are related.

At stake with Noah is the issue of how it could be that this special, righteous, chosen one could turn out to be a drunk in a tent. Once Willis named and then probed the issue, it must have become clear to him that the fundamental turn had to arise somehow out of the covenant embodied in the rainbow. Hence, the *running the story* option was natural. The rainbow is *in* the text itself.

Keck could have used the same narrative option, of course, by beginning with the biblical story of the needy crowd and the self-understood inadequacy of the disciples. Certainly, both the issue and the answer of inadequacy are inside the text, and the students could have been brought into that framework. From this distance I am unable to read his mind as to why he chose to delay the text, but I can say why I might have done what he did. Simply, once the focus is named—namely, inadequacy—the question is, Where is the most powerfully crisp rendering of it? The answer is, with the students. Indeed, it is possible that the on-campus issue prompted the recollection of the text to begin with. The natural result is *delaying the story*.

The "workers in the vineyard" text prompted the issue very clearly and, hence, my naming the focus of injustice early in the preparation process. But the text would not yield any resolution. When that occurred—and after repeated attempts to find the resolution inside the text—I had no option but to look elsewhere for a turn toward resolution. As soon as I started looking elsewhere for the answer (and being hopeful I would finally find one), the sermonic form of *suspending the story* became inevitable.

Saul's persecution of the church (and the bitterness behind it—the *why*) is the issue of the text Craddock employed—the focus. Certainly, it is not the only issue in that passage from Galatians. But it was the one Craddock chose to feature. He must have thought we might know something about the subject. He could have employed the suspension design, beginning with the text and then moving behind it to Saul's background. Or, he could have delayed the use of the text by starting with our bitterness and then moving to Saul. But in either case, he would have made the move only once. He chose to make multiple transitions in and out of the text. Part of that choice may have been suggested by the complication of Saul's journey, as well as by some thought of the prejudiced attitudes we might bring to Saul. The other consideration is that while the focus is prompted by the text, the resolution is not. Craddock's analytical treatment of Saul's internal war provided the sermon's fundamental turn. The kitten story provided the evocation of the good news. What makes the sermon biblical is the bottom line of Craddock's understanding that what is true in the kitten story was already the truth behind the conversion of Saul. It is often the case that when the fundamental turn is provided by logical argument, the freedom of the *alternating the story* form offers important advantages. Notice, too, how clarity in naming sermonic *focus* and *turn* results in clarity about sermonic *aim*. None of these sermons can be reduced to "educational" didactic goals. Willis intended for us to be grasped by God's covenant; Keck aimed for the transforming power of Christ to do something with our inadequacies; Craddock offered not information but cure born of God's love for us, even in our bitterness; and my hope was for the listeners to receive an invitation home.

In summary, I am convinced that when a text is explored thoroughly, with the preacher asking, "What is the focus here?" rather than "What is the message here?" the homiletical work is energized remarkably. Moreover, the question of focus naturally evokes the question about the turn: "How can this issue get resolved, and where is resolution to be found?" "Is it in the text, or before it, or after it, or outside it?" Answers to these questions very quickly and quite naturally will suggest an obvious shape the final message can take. *Running the story, delaying the story, suspending the story,* and *alternating the story* are four basic yet reasonably flexible shapes that narrative sermons may likely take. Once the design question is settled, naming the sermonic aim is greatly facilitated. Often the question of aim is not so much a matter of volition as a matter of recognition—that is, of discovering what it is that the sermon itself seems to be intending to do. Once the sermonic intention is clear, other kinds of preparation steps fall into place.